# LIST OF CO

*Editorial Note:* This edition has been revised in the light of extensive new knowledge, which was unavailable when the book was first published in 1974. The book is illustrated with a mixture of old and 2005 photographs. Captions use present-day or final names only.

It should be noted that this work does not cover clubs, though there have been several in Romsey over the years. Currently, three survive - the Conservative Working Men's Club (in the old *Swan Inn*, Market Place), the British Legion (in Love Lane) and the Old Comrades Club (in The Harrage).

*Acknowledgements:* Several people have again offered information and assistance for this new edition, and their efforts have been much appreciated. Thanks are particularly due to Phoebe Merrick, both as current contributor and as author of the 1974 edition, much of which has been absorbed into this work.

2006 text: Barbara Burbridge
2005 Photographs: Malcolm Heathcote

3

# HAMPSHIRE.

### FREEHOLD INVESTMENT, EQUAL TO A GROUND RENT, WITH REVERSION IN 25 YEARS.

## Particulars and Conditions of Sale

OF A VALUABLE AND IMPORTANT

# FREEHOLD PROPERTY

Situate in and near the Towns of

## ROMSEY & LYMINGTON,

Near SOUTHAMPTON, and about three hours' journey by S. W. Railway from London, and comprising

# The Horsefair Brewery,

## ROMSEY.

With all the Buildings necessary for carrying on the large and well established trade for many years connected therewith, including

BREW-HOUSE, HOP-STORE, 2 LARGE MALT-HOUSES, EXTENSIVE CELLARAGE, &c.,

## A CAPITAL MODERN PRIVATE RESIDENCE,

With GARDEN attached, the whole occupying an area of about

## SIX ACRES

ALSO

# 22 PUBLIC-HOUSES & BEER-HOUSES

Nearly all Freehold, and situate in Romsey and the neighbourhoood and in Lymington, many with

## LARGE GARDENS & MEADOW LAND

Attached, COTTAGES, &c., the whole let on Repairing Lease for a term, of which 25 years are unexpired, at rents amounting to £470 per annum;

### for Sale by Auction by Messrs.

# HARDS, VAUGHAN & JENKINSON

AT THE

AUCTION MART, Tokenhouse Yard, near the Bank of England, London,

## On THURSDAY, MAY the 20th, 1875,

At One for Two o'clock, in ONE LOT,

By direction of the Mortgagee, with the concurrence of the Devisees and Executors under the Will of the late Mrs. CATHERINE HALL.

May be viewed by permission of the Lessee and his under-tenants, and copies of these Particulars and Conditions of Sale, with Plan, may be obtained of Messrs. WHITES, RENARD & Co., Solicitors, Budge Row, Cannon Street, E.C.; at the Auction Mart; at the "White Horse," Romsey; the "Fountain," Portsmouth; the "Dolphin," Southampton; the "Nag's Head," Lymington; and of the Auctioneers, 62, Moorgate Street, London, E.C., and Greenwich, Kent.

On the same day will be sold, with vacant possession, a small Freehold Detached Residence, with about 20 Acres of Land, known as "The Island," Greatbridge, near Romsey, almost entirely surrounded by the River Test, and having the advantage of about a mile of Trout Fishing.

*Sales Particulars for The Horsefair Brewery, 1875*
*(later known as Strong's Brewery)*

4

*"So drunk he must have been to Romsey"*
Old Saying

A History of the Pubs and Inns of Romsey
Compiled and published by
The History Section of the
Lower Test Valley Archaeological Study Group

*Reprinted 1975 and 1982*
**Second Edition 2006**

**ISBN: 0 906921 23 6**

**The Lamb Inn, 7 Mainstone**

The *Lamb* was between the *Horse & Jockey* and the *Bridge Tavern*. This old photograph was not in the LTVAS collection when the first edition of the book was published. The building is now a private house and the bay windows are long since gone.

***The private residence that has replaced the Lamb Inn***

# PREFACE

After the formation of the Lower Test Valley Archaeological Study Group in 1973, the first meeting was addressed by the then County Archivist, Miss Margaret Cash, who spoke about documents and archives. Her talk gave impetus to a group in the audience, whose members were interested in the study of the written word as a major contribution to research. Thus the History Section of the LTVAS Group was born.

Thirteen people attended the inaugural meeting at which the first year's work was decided. Subsequently, a number of other people joined in the work, while others branched out into different areas of archaeological work.

At the first meeting it was planned to spend one year on research of a topic, and then to publish the findings. It was decided to write a history of pubs because there was and is plenty of information about them. Pubs have an important role in any community, and in Romsey there have been so many that work on them would widen into a study of a large number of buildings and families within the town. The inclusion of the village pubs was considered, but it was decided that this would make the work too unwieldy.

It was quickly obvious that one year was not long enough to research even a single topic exhaustively. Nevertheless, it was felt preferable to complete one job of work and then to tackle another, rather than spend five years doing more detailed research on what was, after all, a very limited aspect of Romsey's history.

The History Section had much enjoyment from the work. Members went to libraries, the Archive Office and the Town Hall to make notes from old books and documents. Every existing pub and a large number of ex-pubs were visited, and some of the old deeds studied. Each surviving house was photographed, and extracts were taken from the notes Dr John Latham made for a history of Romsey in 1810.

## Acknowledgements 1974

The Group was particularly grateful to the Romsey Archaeological Research Committee, which made a generous grant in 1973. This funded the purchase of a microfilm reader for studying a film of Dr Latham's notes at the weekly meetings. As well as all the visits, a nucleus of the Section met every Tuesday to classify the information that had been assembled.

A very large number of people helped in the gathering of information. Thanks are due to them, although it is not possible to mention them all by name. The researchers appreciated the contributions of the publicans who made time to talk, to *The Romsey Advertiser* and the *Southern Evening Echo* for the publicity given, and to the many people who wrote to the two newspapers, or directly to LTVAS, with information. The people who gave information will find much of it within these pages; further details about sources are noted in the LTVAS files. Finally, thanks go to the kind people who read through the manuscript and gave their opinion of it.

A VERY
VALUABLE & IMPORTANT FREEHOLD ESTATE,
(A very small part only being Leasehold and Copyhold), consisting of most improvable property, situate in and near the Towns of ROMSEY and LYMINGTON, in the County of Hampshire, within a short distance of Southampton, Portsmouth, the Isle of Wight, Salisbury and Winchester, and about three hours' journey by South Western Railway from London, and comprising

A FREEHOLD BREWERY,
For many years well known in the locality as 'THE HORSEFAIR BREWERY', Romsey, occupying a large site in the centre of the Town, together with all Buildings necessary for carrying on the large and old-established business for many years connected therewith; these are substantial, for the most part built of brick, in excellent repair and consisting of:

A GOOD BREWHOUSE
Of dimensions suitable for the 15qr Plant with which it is fitted.

EXTENSIVE CELLARAGE,
nearly 300 ft long;

*LARGE PALE ALE STORE; a 12-Quarter MALT-HOUSE*
About 110 ft long; a smaller ditto, of two floors;

A LARGE HOP STORE, OF FOUR FLOORS,
DETACHED STABLING,
Comprising two 4-stall Stable and Loose Box, with Loft over; a 4-stall cart-horse Stable, Loose Box, Cow-shed, and open Cart-shed; small Harness Room; Pig-stye; Rick-yard with brick-and-timber Sheds; a brick-and-timber Building, forming Coach-house and Cooper's Shop, Carpenter's Shop over, W.C. in rear.

BRICK-BUILT OFFICES
Consisting of Clerk's Office and Private Room. Spirit Store, Coal-shed.
There is a Well of good water on the Premises
The Brewery is entered from the street known as 'The Horsefair' by a pair of folding gates, and there is a private road leading from the entrance to the main buildings, which lie well in the rear. Close to the entrance gates is a comfortable

*DETACHED MODERN RESIDENCE*
Substantially built of red brick and of pleasing elevation, recently erected by the lessee at a large cost, and containing – On the Ground Floor – Entrance Hall and three good Reception-rooms; on the Upper Floors – four best Bedrooms and two Attics; Kitchens, Dairy, &c. A well-kept Flower Garden in the rear, laid out in lawns and prettily timbered; a good Kitchen Garden, and a

LARGE PADDOCK
Partly bounded by a branch of the river Test, and nearly surrounded by a Belt of Plantation. There are several fine old walnut trees and timber of mature growth.

THESE SPLENDID BREWERY PREMISES
Cover an area of about 6a. 1r. 17p.
As shewn on the plan, and are in the occupation of the Lessee, Mr Thomas Strong, who carries on the business of a Brewer and Maltster, and whose large connection well-earned reputation in the vicinity of Romsey and ten miles round, is too well known to need comment.

*Details of The Horsefair Brewery, 1875*

**Site of the Hundred Bridge at the east end of the Market Place**
*The Holbrook Stream (now underground at this point) marked the demarcation between Romsey Infra and Romsey Extra until 1876. Romsey Corporation could only control drinking places within Romsey Infra. Beyond the bridge, licensing was long the responsibility of another authority.*

## INTRODUCTION

### BACKGROUND
The aim of this work remains as it was in 1974, namely to trace the story of Romsey's historic pubs and to follow the changes in brewing and beer-retailing in Romsey over the centuries. Beer-selling has followed the general pattern of retail businesses, although it has been more strictly controlled than other trades and has always had distinctive features of its own.

In late-20th-century Britain, when this study began, it was easy to regard earlier Romsonians as somewhat decadent with their use of beer as a regular drink. It should be remembered, however, that water and milk had only become clean and safe in modern times, and that for many centuries beer, which must be boiled in production, was a safer drink.

### THE EARLY STORY: Before the 19th Century
#### Ale and Beer
Hops were added to beer in this country from 1480. Before then, the brew was based on barley. The unhopped brew was ale, and the hopped drink was called beer. Gradually, beer overtook ale because of its better keeping qualities, and drinkers learned to prefer the flavour. Later, the distinction between ale and beer became blurred.

7

As brewing evolved, so did certain ancillary businesses keep pace. Encouraged by the need for local ingredients, growers used small fields in and around the town as hop gardens. The name of 'hop gardens' was still attached to several small fields in the 19th century. By then, however, the name was all that survived. Brewers had found it more economic to buy their hops on a much larger scale than local growers could provide.

Malt-houses, too, once abounded, often associated with bakers' premises. Some of them seem to have been constructed of mud 'cob'. Eventually, these also disappeared from the Romsey scene as the emerging larger breweries built their own malt-houses.

## Types of Drinking Places

A range of drinking places evolved over time, all strictly controlled in theory, although unlicensed premises were a perennial problem. The three types were ale-houses, taverns and inns. The ale-house was the most basic, selling only ale or beer. Next in the hierarchy was the tavern, which might sell wine as well as ale and beer. Most towns were limited to one each, but there were some exceptions to this rule. London was allowed forty; Salisbury and Southampton three each. It is tempting to speculate which house in Romsey was the official tavern.

For a business to qualify as an inn - the most prestigious hostelry - the landlord had to provide beds, food and stabling besides the full range of alcoholic refreshment. In 1618, Sir Giles Mompesson had a patent to license inns, and only sixty-seven were so licensed in Hampshire. Unfortunately, it has not been possible to find the list, but any inn would need a large site with a spacious building and ample space for stables and a coachyard. There are several candidates for Romsey's earliest inn, particularly in the Market Place. The *White Horse* and the *Swan* are probably the most likely.

Romsey, undoubtedly, always had plenty of pubs of various sorts, for it was not only the local people who looked for refreshment there. The town was situated on important routes - from Winchester to the West of England, and from the wool-producing areas of Wiltshire to the port of Southampton. The medieval woollen-cloth trade was the basis of Romsey's wealth for many centuries, and the cloth entrepreneurs brought business to the publicans. A growing prosperity attracted a variety of craftsmen to support the population. And besides the trades people, there were travellers using the town as a convenient resting point. The weekly market also attracted both outsiders and local inhabitants to the town centre.

When the Abbey was a flourishing institution, the monastic precinct was a virtual village in its own right. It has been suggested that such a religious establishment would have needed some four or five servants for every nun. Visitors came to see the nuns, their priests, the Abbey steward and the lesser staff; craftsmen came to help with the continual building programme within the precinct. All would have needed accommodation and refreshment. Although the Abbey brewed a supply of beer for its own consumption and as part payment to various officials, the town hostelries

8

undoubtedly benefited from the presence of the array of itinerants drawn to Romsey by its Benedictine nunnery.

## Local Authorities and the Licensing Regulations

From the earliest times, those in authority - at both Parliamentary and local level - felt the need to control the sale of ale or beer, partly as a source of revenue and partly in the interests of law and order.

For some 600 years the Abbess ruled both Abbey and Romsey Infra. But everything changed after the dissolution of the Abbey in 1539. In the mid-16th century, Parliamentary law made it necessary to have a licence signed by two Justices of the Peace before a business could be set up.

Romsey Corporation officially controlled the affairs of the Borough from the time of the 1607 Charter, granted by James I. Even before then, a Mayor and Constables had ordered the affairs of the town. However, it must be remembered that the Borough created in 1607 was very small, and continued to be so for a long time. The western boundary was the River Test, as at present, but the eastern boundary was the Town Stream – the Holbrook - that can be seen running north-south through the Lortemore Place car park and then, after passing underground for a stretch, emerging alongside the Bus Station and through Duke's Mill. When the stream was completely open, there used to be a bridge across it at the junction between the Market Place and The Hundred. In medieval times it was called Broad Bridge, but subsequently became the Hundred Bridge. (The names Romsey Infra and Romsey Extra refer to this bridge, which long marked the boundary between the two. Places were either *infra pontem*, meaning 'inside the bridge', or *extra pontem*, meaning 'outside the bridge'.)

Romsey's first town hall was just within the historic Borough adjacent to the north side of this one-time bridge (It is now 23 Market Place). The Corporation met on the first floor with the ground floor serving as the constable's base, complete with cells on the damp stream side. If the 20th-century façade is ignored, and the side of the building studied, the age of the property may be better appreciated. The overall shape of the building is unchanged, and the side doorway through which Corporation members entered to reach their Council Chamber still exists.

It was in this upper Chamber that the drinking regulations were administered for the pubs in Romsey Infra. Those in Romsey Extra were under the jurisdiction of the Hundred of King's Somborne. In fact, most of the pubs in the survey spent the greater part of their lives in Romsey Extra until Romsey Infra began to expand after 1876.

From the start, the Borough, like Parliament, maintained its twin aims when controlling the pubs. On the one hand, councillors used hostelries as a source of revenue via licensing fees, and on the other hand they recognised the need to regulate drinking and ensure the behaviour of customers. The keeping of order also fell into two parts. Both the drinkers and the retailers

9

had to be kept in order.  An additional general consideration was the health of the local economy, which was ensured by protecting all existing trade.

So, as well as seeking to generate revenue, the authorities devised regulations to protect the livelihoods of local townspeople, and to prevent impecunious outsiders becoming dependent on the Poor Rates.  Outsiders might be allowed to trade in the town only if they paid a deposit.  There was, for example, the case of an 18th-century shoemaker whose business failed after some years.  His £5 deposit was returned to him.  By 1800, this practice of making a deposit had been relaxed.  The result was that, when a certain blacksmith came to Romsey, failed in business and then died, his wife and seven children became destitute.  If he had had to lodge a deposit with the Corporation first, there would have been a buffer to protect his family and the Poor Rates.  There are no accounts of victuallers falling on hard times in similar vein, although there is no reason to think that all licensees were successful.  Dickman, at the *Spotted Dog* in 1785, gave up after one year and was reduced to taking a job as a Post Boy in Alresford.

The Corporation's control of victuallers may have been just one part of its general regulation of all trade, but, amongst all the local relevant controls, the sale of pub licences and the regulation of the liquor trade were regarded as especially important.

Regulations devised in the 17th century continued and evolved into the 18th century, even though, like the deposit, some requirements had somewhat fallen into disuse by 1800.  In 1709, the Constables' Report recorded 'We present Joseph James, John Kent and Steven Rolph for retailing ale without licences'; so the law in Romsey was keeping a strict eye on individuals trading illegally even though such efforts did not always succeed.  In 1742, the Corporation clearly felt that further tightening of controls was needed.  It was specified that 'no person shall sell ale, beer, cider, brandy or other excisable liquor without licence as above under penalty of 10/-'.  The Aldermen of the Wards and the Tythingmen (in each tything or ward) were made responsible for seeing that the law was upheld and for reporting to the Town Hall, on Court Days, the names of any defaulters.

**Romsey's Licensed Premises**
The Corporation allowed only six official ale-houses within the Borough. They had great difficulty in enforcing this rule, which suggests they may have fixed the number of houses too low.  Certainly, the large number of pubs of all sorts found in Romsey Extra, immediately beyond the Borough boundaries, does endorse this idea.

To the west, most of these Romsey Extra pubs were in a tightly packed stretch extending from lower Middlebridge Street across the River Test into Mainstone.  These pubs had the double advantage of catching traffic from the New Forest area and also from Salisbury, once the Southampton-Salisbury turnpike trust had created the new link over Green Hill to Whiteparish.  (Previously, traffic to Salisbury had to go through north

Greatbridge and thence over Awbridge Common, meeting up with the Whiteparish road at Shootash.)

Curiously, some major routes to the east did not attempt to lure travellers in similar fashion. While pubs were crowded into the central Romsey Extra streets, such as The Hundred and Latimer Street, not one pub has been identified for Botley Road, the turnpike road to Portsmouth. Cupernham Lane was also devoid of pubs. Although not a turnpike, it played an important role as the bad weather alternative way north, via Yokesford Hill, whenever the causeway to Greatbridge was subject to the winter floods that were typical of that area.

### The Victualler
Early victuallers were expected to have served a five- or seven-year apprenticeship, and then had to buy licences from the Mayor. The price of beer remained fairly static throughout the 18$^{th}$ century, but the cost of becoming a licensee did not. In 1710, the national fee for a victualling licence had been only 1s 0d, but in 1804 the cost rose to two guineas (£2 2s 0d). This seemed to contradict Parliament's desire to divert the poor from gin to beer by making the acquisition of a beer licence less difficult. Presumably, it was hoped that higher fees would discourage the less reputable licensees.

The numerous pubs in Romsey Extra did not inhibit people from opening unofficial establishments within the Borough. Problems with such unlicensed drinking places are indicated by the fines imposed on the lawbreakers. In 1668, the standard fine for selling beer without a licence from the Mayor was 26d, a sum more normally presented as 2s 2d. In 1687, however, five people were each fined 20s 0d (£1) for selling beer without a licence. The Corporation seems to have been resorting to swingeing penalties, possibly for persistent offenders at least.

In the rules of 1668, the Corporation re-emphasised the general licensing policy, directing that 'no person within the town shall sell except licensed by the Mayor'. In addition, victuallers had to renew their licences annually, find two sureties of £5 apiece and take a poor boy or girl apprentice.

### The Pauper Apprentice
Needless to say, the pauper apprentice scheme had its drawbacks. The idea was that the victuallers were able to teach these apprentices the trade, helping them to become self-sufficient. During the apprenticeship, the victualler would support the child, thus effecting a saving to the Poor Rates. In practice, apprentice and master did not always agree. In 1670, it was ordered that 'Elizabeth Loder, apprentice to John Hawke, be sent home to him again and he ordered to receive her and in the meantime she was absent from him being two months, to pay 10/- to the mother for the relief of the daughter during that time'. It is possible that John Hawke was John Hacke of the *Bell Inn* where he prospered and issued his own trade tokens.

11

The pauper apprentice scheme was dropped in 1742, by which time the drawbacks had made it unviable. Nevertheless, the Borough had been following an accepted pattern of behaviour when it apprenticed these poor children to victuallers.

And, although the official system regarding paupers was scrapped after 1742, parents still put their children out to work with victuallers. A man named Henry Butt, talking in 1804, could tell the Mayor of his own experience, although unlike Elizabeth Loder he does not seem to have been unhappy – or unfortunate - with his lot. He had entered service with Joseph Jenvey of Romsey Infra, a wine merchant, and his father was paid a weekly sum for his services. After three years, Mr Jenvey died and young Butt made a new arrangement with Mr Jenvey's son, who took over the business. Butt became his servant in exchange for board, lodging and a livery suit. When Butt left to join the Supplementary Militia, Mr Jenvey gave him 'two suits of clothes and half a crown'.

**Murder of a Victualler**
Perhaps the most dramatic incident relating to a Romsey licensee was really a domestic rather than a trade-related crime. It was nothing less than the murder of an innkeeper, William Ives. In the late 17th century he kept a victualling house 'known by the sign of the *Hatchet*', which may have been on the corner of old Newton Lane, probably on the north side.

William's wife, Esther, had a lover, John Noyse, a Wellow man 'by Trade a Cooper but a person of ill Fame and a very Desolate Liver'. On 5th November 1686, the lovers murdered William Ives, but the cries of the victim and the couple's children were overheard by the nightwatchman, who fetched the town constable. The lovers were literally caught red-handed with the victim's blood upon them. After being found guilty at a trial in Winchester, they were returned to Romsey, where they were imprisoned in the town hall cells while waiting to be executed. It is recorded that the pair were executed in the Market Place but the exact spot is unknown, though it was probably close to the town hall of the time (now 23 Market Place).

John Noyse was hanged, but Esther was doomed to an even more harrowing fate. As an adulterous murdering wife, she had been sentenced to death by burning. She received a special concession in that the executioner was ordered to strangle her prior to the flames being lit – a gruesome end to a gruesome story, the whole tale being recorded in a cautionary pamphlet.

**To Keep an Orderly House**
William Ives lived at a time when the Corporation was trying to maintain law and order in the town's various hostelries. A key restriction placed on victuallers in the 17th century, and one that continues to this day, was the responsibility laid on them to keep an orderly house. Historically, this also included observance of the restricted opening and closing hours, particularly the rule that forbade the selling of alcohol during church services.

There are early references to ale-house keepers and innkeepers being bound in the sum of '£10 to keep peace and good order and suffer no tippling during Divine Service'. In 1670, William Ireland of the *Falcon* appears to have failed in his innkeeping duties as he was bound in the sum of 10s 0d to appear at the next Sessions 'to answer for keeping idle persons in his house who threw out a chamber pot or a glass of beer on the Mayor and Company going to Church Service'.

During the 18<sup>th</sup> century the control of drinkers and licensees continued much as before, still with special restrictions on drinking during Church services. In 1746, George Pocock and Edw. Hore were fined for 'resorting to a public drinking house called the *Black Swan* of a Sunday during Divine Service'.

Despite the disapproving attitude towards those who drank at forbidden times, there are surprisingly few recorded cases of people being charged with drunkenness alone. In 1683, however, two men were fined 5s 0d apiece for being common drunkards. Their names were Will Gunson the younger, and William Sanger the older. They must have been great nuisances for these were very heavy fines, and such penalties were not very common.

**Side Regulations**
Over time, there were various side regulations of the drinking trade that affected licensees. The Corporation regulated weights and measures and, in 1670, spent 14s 0d on a new gallon measure and on 'trying' the old one. In 1692, indictments were made for the selling of beer and ale in unsealed pots and flagons. Dr Latham, writing in 1810, recorded that, for many years, pegs were introduced into tankards, and anyone who drank below the peg incurred a penalty. The reasoning behind this rule was that, if people drank too low, they disturbed the sediment that would have collected because the beer was not in those times cleared by the use of finings. Unfortunately, Dr Latham did not produce any evidence for this 'peg' practice in Romsey.

**Beer and the Economy**
As well as keeping control over trade generally and licensing laws in particular, the authorities were also observant about the price of beer, as this had economic significance. Because of the technicalities of brewing, fewer people made their own beer than baked their own bread - so the price of beer was a very important item in the cost of living. During the 18<sup>th</sup> century the price of strong beer was stable at 3d a quart from 1722 to 1760, and at 3½d from 1760 to 1799, when wars with the French disturbed the equilibrium. Until 1799, brewers had been able to balance good years against bad ones, and to make a profit overall. It must also be remembered that there were more acres under barley (used in brewing) than under wheat (used for flour), so barley and beer were both of major economic importance.

Parliament, too, appreciated the revenue accrued from taxes levied on barley malt. There was a generally perceived need for the quality of beer as the national drink to be maintained.

## THE LATER STORY: After 1800
### Beer versus Gin

Beer's significance to the economy was only one aspect of the favour it won with the authorities. During the 18th century, beer had also begun to be seen as a worthy alternative to the worrying consumption of gin, so graphically recorded by Hogarth, the artist. In order to combat excessive gin-drinking among the lower orders, and as part of the drive against the recognised evils of gin-drinking, Parliament determined to make gin expensive and beer of easier access.

There is no evidence that gin drinking was a great problem in Romsey, but Parliament was, inevitably, more concerned with London, where gin-drinking was having a disastrous effect. At the end of the 18th century, the Justices had been given much more control over licensed premises, and a Royal Proclamation on vice and immorality led to the worst houses being closed. The Borough of Romsey Infra already seemed to have considerable control over premises in the town but the new laws undoubtedly made for greater control in Romsey Extra.

From 1830, any householder assessed for the payment of the Poor Rate could obtain an Excise Licence to retail beer for sale on or off the premises. The number of beer houses in Romsey throughout the 19th century seems to indicate that beer-retailing remained a popular venture despite the cost of obtaining a licence. Unfortunately, as long as the necessary money was available, licences could be obtained with such ease that the trade quickly became overcrowded. Although licensees could sell liquor any time between 4am and 10pm except during Divine Service on Sundays, Good Friday and Christmas Day, they were seldom able to earn enough money. They therefore felt obliged to serve all customers no matter how disorderly. The rise in the cost of the licence had not had the desired effect on standards.

Nevertheless, the authorities seem to have continued with this form of control, and, in 1834, the price of a licence was raised again, this time to three guineas (£3 3s 0d). Additionally, the granting of a licence was then also made subject to a good character reference signed by six rated inhabitants of the Parish. In 1840, a further restriction meant that licence holders had to prove they were resident holders or occupiers of the houses for which they wanted a licence. This stopped the practice whereby one acceptable person could hold several licences, sometimes as a 'cover' for undesirable people.

All the restrictive rules previously laid down by the Corporation of Romsey had been overtaken by new laws. Instead of a few licensed victuallers, there were now a vast number, as the Appendix shows. There were so many that few could make a living solely by selling beer. Many of them had other trades, often in building or farming, or were employed in full-time jobs with family members running the licensed premises. The role of women is particularly highlighted by the number of widows who kept on the licence after their husbands' death.

Apart from falling foul of licensing regulations, victuallers sometimes found themselves in trouble with the law for one or two other reasons. The less responsible landlords might, like mine-host of the *Royal Oak* in 1837, be caught selling beer after hours; or they might; knowingly or not, find their premises being used in the handling of stolen goods.

**Drinking Places and Behaviour**
On 5th October 1829, a Court decree determined that a special session for the transfer of alehouse licences 'pursuant to the directions of 9th Geo. Cap. 61' should be held on the first Saturday in December next, the first Saturday in March next, the first Saturday in June next and the first Saturday in August. There was obviously a determination to keep the issuing of liquor licences under regular review.

By the 19th century, however, there were quite a few small ale-houses around the town, and it seems that some of them were not properly controlled, even if licensed. Inevitably, perhaps, many of those attracted to drinking places were on the wrong side of the law, if only in a minor way.

In June 1838, the landlord of the *Cross Keys*, James Liddle, claimed that Jonathan and Maria Paddock, who had slept at his house, stole two shawls and a waistcoat. Maria Paddock was the culprit, her husband reportedly in ignorance of her actions. Sometimes it was the landlord himself who was the guilty party. John Carden, beer-seller, was himself implicated in a theft of clothes worth 50s 0d. The victim suggested that some of her lost goods were hidden in his house.

Carden's ale-house was frequently in trouble. In January 1837, James Harding, watchman on duty in Bell Street, was approached by a Mrs Summers, who asked him to 'go and clear Carden's beer shop' as her husband was there. Another watchman, James Viney, said that Carden's Middlebridge Street shop had been open after hours. Although Carden protested that he had been having a private party, he was fined 40s 0d with 10s 0d costs.

Indeed, Middlebridge Street seems to have been an undisciplined area in respect of its beer shops. Another beer-seller there, by the name of John Webb, was found by Constable Pearce at 11pm on a Saturday night with 20 people in his tap room drinking beer and 'a man named Handcock with some cards in his hand'. Webb was fined 40s 0d with 8s 0d costs.

The *Vine* in Cherville Street, on the other hand, was in trouble in 1838 for serving drinks before opening time. The ever-vigilant Constable Pearce found Gear, the landlord, drinking with two men in the kitchen. Gear claimed that they were lodgers who had just come in, but he was fined £1 12s 0d including costs.

During the 19th century, there were many assaults on men and women, and these attacks were often fuelled by alcohol. A disastrous incident was reported in *The Hampshire Chronicle* of 22nd November 1851. It resulted in the death of a Minstead farmer, who had come to Romsey on business. The full report is included in the supplement to this introduction (page 23).

## The Temperance Movement

It was only after 1830 that the effects of beer-drinking became a major concern, giving impetus to the Temperance Movement. Once water (or tea) became reasonable alternatives to beer, then opposition got under way. Until then beer had been seen as a normal drink, and spirits were the enemy, but the blame that had once been heaped upon gin was now transferred to beer.

There was a strong Temperance Movement in Romsey, boosted by the large number of Nonconformists in the town. Even so, some Nonconformist grocers felt able to sell alcoholic drinks as part of their trade, and the influential Purchase family were hop factors and maltsters, although they did not brew beer. On a minor level, it is recorded that for many years, the boiling water for the Temperance teas was supplied by a local brewery.

Having actively encouraged widespread beer-drinking and retailing, Parliament had to legislate to redress the balance, bringing the situation under control while still enabling publicans to make a living from their trade. It was a long time, however, before the Temperance Movement could relax.

Coincidentally, changes in the law were reinforced by secondary controls evolving from the growth of commercial brewing from the 18th century onwards. This growth gradually affected the role of the victualler, turning most into retailers only.

## Growth of the Common Brewer

Changes in the brewing trade had a great impact on all aspects of the business. Originally, all or nearly all licensees had brewed their own beer. Gradually, some houses found it economic to buy the beer for resale, while others had turned to making more beer than they could sell direct, and so had begun to supply other retailers. In 1700, half of all beer sold had been home-brewed, but in 1800 the figure had dropped to one third. At that time, though, the market was shared between a number of small but competitive breweries; it would be very difficult to forecast which of several businesses might become paramount in an area.

During the 19th century, both Parliament and the larger common breweries gained much tighter control of the licensed victuallers. Almost accidentally, breweries began to own licensed premises. When their cash flow was good, they were in a position to lend money to publicans, enjoying the benefits of repayments during leaner financial periods.

The nature of brewing was such that commercial brewers (or common brewers as they were called) spent much money buying in raw materials at harvest time. At this point they might need to borrow money. They would then brew for nine months until the weather became unsuitable, at which

16

point they would take stock and rest.   After the Annual Stocktaking, the senior men would receive their annual salary, plus bonuses in a good year.

Once their raw materials had been bought in the autumn, the brewers' outgoings would be low since most of their employees were low-paid manual labourers.   Generally their cash flow was such that, for most of the year, brewers had a steady high income with low expenditure.   Therefore, they had a good deal of idle money that they could lend to others.   Indeed, some large-scale brewing and banking families were closely linked.

At first the brewers simply demanded that those publicans to whom they loaned money should buy their beer exclusively.   They were not seriously interested in 'tying' houses through ownership, but whenever their debtors defaulted, they were more or less forced to foreclose and acquire the houses.   Altogether, they were in a prime position to purchase pubs and inns.   They began to realise that this gave them an added security.   The acquisition of pubs gave them a real advantage over rivals.

Ownership became a positive policy, a process made easier by the way in which brewing income accrued during most months of the year.   In 1800, the heirs of J. Galpin owned several houses, and Trodd and Hall, an early example of an expanding brewery business, owned the *Vine Inn*, the *Star*, the *Lord Nelson* and the *Sun Inn* at least.   At that time, the Trodd and Hall brewery, though significant, was far from holding even a local monopoly.   The Latham Brewery, for example, challenged them in the twenty or so years prior to 1817.

**The Common Brewer and the Transport System**
Beer requires smooth transport if it is to retain its quality.   The poor transport systems of early centuries meant that brewers were contained within a radius of some fifteen or sixteen miles.   This was restricting in small towns such as Romsey with a limited population.   In the 18th century, however, the brewers in densely populated areas had been able to exploit the brewing of porter (a dark brown, bitter beer), which was a large-scale operation.   This had brought about a metamorphosis in their finances, and they had become true capitalists.   Brewers in an area of small population like Romsey, though, could not benefit from these developments, but continued to be financed on a small scale as a cottage industry.

First the turnpike roads of the 18th century and then, more importantly, the rail network of the mid-19th century improved transport and gradually changed the picture completely.   Beer could be carried increasingly further without harm, and brewers started to encroach on each others' traditional preserves.   Immediately, the whole industry turned into large-scale capitalist enterprises, with the less successful being driven out of business or bought out by their rivals.

In order to sell his beer, the successful brewer must acquire as many retail outlets as possible and then control them for the good of the company's reputation.   By the early 19th century, brewers were already continually

17

checking publicans to make sure that the beer they were selling was neither flat nor watered nor adulterated. It was important also that pubs were not retailing the beer of rival firms. This was when enterprising brewers realised they would have an edge over competitors if they began to tie houses as a matter of policy. There were still financial pitfalls to be avoided, however, and some apparently successful businesses failed after a while.

John Latham was the Romsey brewer who illustrated this situation. Buying into an existing business in the 1790s, he quickly realised the wider advantages of tied houses. Proof of this is found in the 1817 list of some eighteen pubs that he owned. Unfortunately, the reason for this list was the need of his bankruptcy assignees to know what they had to dispose of over the next two or three years. The Latham 'empire' had extended westwards as far as Lymington, northwards up the Test Valley to Houghton and eastwards to Winchester and Bishops Waltham. But John Latham did not have enough capital to sustain his enterprise. Rashly over-reaching himself, he mortgaged and deceitfully re-mortgaged his property until creditors' demands brought the whole edifice tumbling down. (This John Latham, incidentally, was the son of the Dr John Latham who recorded so much of Romsey's early history and who was personally ruined by his son's disaster.)

John Latham's was not the only brewing business to crumble, and while others did survive, their ability to grow was still limited within a local market, and as time went on they became easy prey to take-over bids, leaving just a handful of common brewers controlling most of the pubs between them.

### The Railway & the End of the Coaching Era
The brewers and the pubs had responded to the increase in travel that had developed since the mid-18th century. The new turnpike road system, which had improved the speed and comfort of travel, encouraged more people to undertake long journeys across the country. Whether using public or private coaches, travellers needed places for rest and refreshment. Romsey was at the hub of a network of turnpikes, and many Romsey pubs dated from this era; they enjoyed good business for some 80 or so years.

Then came the railways, the first line – from Bishopstoke to Salisbury – opening in 1847, and the second – from Andover to Southampton - in the 1860s. A railway station serving both lines was built beyond the fields on the town's eastern edge. Long distance travellers, who flocked to this new mode of transport, no longer needed to come into the centre of Romsey, and the local inns suffered as the coaching trade diminished dramatically. Many service trades had depended on coaching, and they suffered along with the inns themselves. Only the market that used the rail system to move livestock benefited from the local railways. Romsey's economy stalled.

### Consolidation
As the 19th century progressed many of the smaller breweries went out of business, leaving the field to fewer and larger concerns. By 1875, sales particulars reveal that one of the survivors, The Horsefair Brewery, had

twenty-two pubs in Hampshire. Already, though, one of the Romsey pubs owned by The Horsefair Brewery – the *Bell Inn* – had ceased to operate, losing its coaching trade to the railways. Other premises in the town suffered a similar fate.

The sale of The Horsefair Brewery was held following the death of Mrs Catherine Hall of The Island, Greatbridge. She was the widow of Charles John Hall, brewer, and the brewery and its associated pubs formed only a part of her estate. The existing lessee of The Horsefair Brewery was Thomas Strong, a name that was to resound around Romsey for a very long time, though in a different form. (See details of The Horsefair Brewery sale on pages 4 and 6.)

In the late 1880s, moderate-sized companies such as The Horsefair Brewery, together with George's Brewery in Bell Street and Jesser & Cressey's Brewery in The Hundred succumbed to the purchasing power of incomer David Faber. He had the acumen to appreciate the potential of the rail network to enlarge his market. He created Strong and Co. of Romsey Ltd, the eventual local super-brewery that straightaway controlled ten houses within Romsey alone. Soon, the 'Strong Country' influence came to be felt County-wide.

With the development of large-scale operations, the few inns that had steadfastly 'brewed their own' found it less economic to compete: a large number gave up brewing and became mere retailers of beer. Among the last to brew in Romsey, Cave at the *Red Lion* and Holloway at the *Woolpack* had ceased operations by 1900, but Smith in Love Lane continued until 1926. The other breweries in the town were bought out or had closed down, leaving Strong and Co. Ltd supreme under David Faber. Only outside breweries, particularly from Winchester, attempted to compete.

**The old Cross Keys, 11 Bell Street**
*Although the Cross Keys pub has been long closed, this sign survives along the side of the building*

## Rationalisation

After the victory was won, then came the rationalisation. Once Strong & Co. Ltd had gained control of most of the retail beer outlets in the town, it became possible to close many pubs in order to make the remainder economically viable. This was the trend of the 20th century.

Such rationalisation was not peculiar to the licensed trade but shared by all retailing. Many houses had devoted one room to a shop where a small range of goods was sold, mainly to neighbours. These little shops were driven out of business because their proprietors could not offer the competitive prices or the range of goods that shoppers came to expect. They were unable to afford the storage and display facilities of bigger shops with more capital, and they went quietly out of business. Only a few individual retail businesses, mainly those with a niche market, managed to survive into the 21st century.

Much beer retailing was once of the same order as this type of shop-keeping. A barrel or so of beer would be bought, racked up in the front room and dispensed to a modest number of customers. The money earned would supplement the family income but did no more than that. The most modest establishment of all was probably Poplar Cottage in The Causeway. This place had a bush licence on fair days only. (Romsey used to have three fairs a year.) The inhabitants of the cottage might hang out a bush or a branch and could then legally sell beer for the stated period. In a sense, this type of licence has returned in the 21st century with the need for occasional licences to be bought for specific functions, such as fetes, at which alcohol may change hands for money, however indirectly (e.g. at a tombola stall).

Meanwhile, most full-time pubs were tied by 1900, and the 1904 Balfour Licensing Act greatly helped the breweries to close a large number of them. This Act gave protection to all existing licences except in the case of misconduct, structural unsuitability or unfitness of the licensee. Any licence protected by the Act could only be extinguished if compensation were paid to the owner, the brewery and the licensee. The money was to come from within the trade itself in the form of a levy on existing licences and a surcharge on new licences. The fund was popularly known as the Brewers' Endowment Fund, or the Mutual Burial Fund. It was in existence until 1959 and undoubtedly did much to speed the closure of many houses, although most of the smaller unnamed beer houses had already vanished by 1900.

A few years passed before the Act took effect in Romsey, and then the closure of seven houses was proposed in 1911. At that time, the town had one pub for every 151.5 people, nearly twice the national average. It was the year that the Temperance lobby reached its zenith in Parliament, but the closures in Romsey seem to have been arranged by the Trade and not by a Romsey Bench in the hands of aggressive teetotallers. Of the seven licences in question, only one gained a reprieve. That was the *Sawyers Arms*, which was the only tied house of the last independent brewer in Romsey, Smith of Love Lane, who claimed his brewing business would not be viable without it.

20

Of the other six houses, three belonged to Strong's - the *Lansdowne Arms*, the *Bridge Tavern* and the *Delve Beer House*. The *Woolpack* and the *Rose & Crown* belonged to the Lion Brewery of Winchester, and one, the *Queens Head* in Bell Street, belonged to the Winchester Brewery. The Winchester brewers commented that it seemed somewhat unfair but doubtless matters were no fairer in their home territory. Two of the Lion Brewery's three Romsey houses were closed that year.

### Strong & Co. Ltd of Romsey

By the late 1920s, Strong's Brewery owned twenty pubs in Romsey - the *Angel*, the *Bishop Blaize*, the *Bricklayers Arms*, the *Cross Keys*, the *Crown*, the *Dolphin*, the *Fleming Arms*, the *Horse and Jockey*, the *Kings Head*, the *Latimer Arms*, the *Railway View*, the *Red Lion*, the *Sawyers Arms*, the *Star*, the *Sun*, the *Three Tuns*, the *Vine*, the *William IV*, the *Hunters Inn* and the *Dukes Head*. Following the Balfour Act, the brewery had already closed down a number of tied houses including the *Lansdowne Arms* (1911), the *Bridge Tavern* (1911), the *Delve Inn* (1911), the *Newton Arms* (1918) and the *Thatched Cottage* (1918).

The chairman and joint managing director of Strong's Brewery in the 1930s, R.C. Chambers, was also involved in local politics. At the outbreak of war, he was the mayor of Romsey and – as happened everywhere while elections were suspended for the duration – remained in that office throughout the conflict. Under his management, Strong & Co. Ltd played a newsworthy role in the war effort in its final year.

In July 1944, the 2nd Tactical Air Force used Spitfires to fly supplies of Strong's beers to the troops in Normandy. The authorities turned a blind eye while casks were suspended from each wing by means of adapted wing fittings. These were listed as 'XXX Depth Charge Fitment'. The exercise was a good morale booster and a splendid piece of advertising for the brewery.

In 1974, the story of Strong & Co. Ltd entered a new phase as Whitbread Wessex Ltd took over the business, and Romsey was no longer the focus of a local brewing empire but simply part of a much more widespread one.

At the time of the takeover, Whitbreads had only eleven tied houses in Romsey. These were the *Angel*, the *Dolphin*, the *Dukes Head*, the *Fleming Arms*, the *Hunters Inn*, the *Kings Head*, the *Red Lion*, the *Star*, the *Sun*, the *Three Tuns* and the *William IV*. There were five other non-Whitbread houses in the town, these being the *Abbey Hotel*, the *Tudor Rose*, the *Phoenix*, the *White Horse Hotel*, and the *Old House at Home*, making a total of sixteen pubs, all but three of which were in the centre of town.

In the following decades, the *Angel*, the *Dolphin*, the *Fleming Arms*, the *Kings Head* and the *Red Lion* ceased to be pubs by the end of the 20th century, though the buildings survive in new incarnations as restaurants, offices or estate agents, or, in the case of the *Dolphin*, as part of a large department store. The breweries were quick to cull the pubs but much slower to provide new ones on the expanding residential estates.

## Conclusion

It is to be hoped that rationalisation will not result in the closure of too many more houses. Romsey's historic reputation for having so many pubs had led to the saying that a person was 'so drunk he must have been to Romsey'. With a much lower number of pubs today, the old adage has lost much of its former strength.

Realising that a pub always stands or falls by the personality of its landlord, the researchers of the early 1970s visited all those pubs still open at the time. They were impressed by the friendliness of Romsey's pubs and how each one seemed to have its own niche in Romsey society. Between the two editions of this book the landlords have remained friendly, but customers' choice has been reduced as more of Romsey's pubs have closed. Against this tide of closures, however, there has been one major introduction to the story of Romsey's pubs. This was the opening of a new one, *Luzborough House*, in a former farmhouse that was once part of the Broadlands estate. It was converted into a pub in 1986.

Since the 1970s, the traditional English pub has had to contend with the rival attractions of licensed restaurants and night clubs. Although some pubs have converted to being licensed restaurants, others have evolved on more traditional lines in response to this challenge. Greater emphasis has been placed on the food offered. Non-alcoholic drinks, even coffee, are now more spontaneously available. Attractive gardens have proliferated where appropriate, and in this respect the country pub often has an advantage over the urban one, and is thus able to cater more easily for young family groups. With private transport commonly at the disposal of anyone from seventeen years old upwards, the 'local' is no longer frequented solely by those who live in its vicinity.

The more flexible opening hours introduced at the end of the 20th and in the early 21st century have also widened the scope –and the responsibilities - of the English pub. Romsey publicans have taken positive action and formed a PubWatch in conjunction with the police. They are in constant communication with each other, and have inspired other retailers to set up a comparable system of information exchange and advice.

Sadly, though, by the beginning of the 21st century, the 'glory days' of Romsey's brewing industry had faded into history. Although The Hampshire Brewery, founded in 1992, had relocated to Romsey in 1997, the town had lost awareness of its splendid brewing history. In gradual stages, Whitbreads had withdrawn from the town towards the end of the 20th century. Present inhabitants no longer have their nostrils assailed by the regular smell of hops during the week. These smells, intermingling with the sweet aromas from the jam factory and the less appetising odours of the Gas Company, hung on the air and were part of the general town atmosphere for many generations. Their departure meant also an acute change of direction for the workforce of the town.

**The Hampshire Chronicle of 22nd November 1851:**

'On Thursday, 13th November, John Soffe, about 55 of Minstead, remarkably healthy and cheerful but addicted to habits of intemperance, drove into Romsey to get some corn ground at the Town Mill. When he did not return his brothers the next day inquired and found he had collected the flour at 4pm. A hat had been found in the River between the Bridge and Sadlers Mill and an empty canvas purse, both belonging to him, on the Saturday.

'On Sunday morning his body was found lying at the bottom of the river near a place called Pearce's meadow about 30 yards above the Millhead. The body was taken to the *Lamb Inn* where the pockets were searched and found to contain nothing of value. A post mortem was ordered by the Coroner and the inquest fixed for Tuesday. A warrant was issued for John Eyres and John Kemish, two of the persons last seen in his company. The post mortem was carried out by Mr Wiltshire, surgeon. There was no trace of external violence or disease, except that the brain and lungs were congested as in cases of suffocation, therefore death was by drowning. At the inquest there were suspicions against Emma Leach and Mary Ann Sims also. The inquest was adjourned to the next day at the Town Hall. There was a large crowd, including the Mayor. Voluminous depositions were taken. When John Soffe paid 2/3 at the mill for the grinding of his corn the miller saw that he had gold and silver in his purse. He then returned to Baileys, tied his horse to the railings and resumed his seat in the tap room, was joined by the prisoners and ordered beer. The landlord, seeing the condition he was in tried to dissuade him from having more, but his companions urged him to have some more. Leach was saying aloud she would leave him. The landlord helped him into his cart and offered to mind his purse, but this was refused. He promised to go straight home.

'The two females followed him asking for more beer, and he pulled up and went into the *Bridge Tavern* (kept by W. Webb) with all four. The two females helped him from his cart. More beer was ordered. Eyres asked for 1/- for binding some leather, done previously, and became very noisy. The landlord threatened to eject him. About six o'clock the two females left. The Deceased left 5 minutes after. Eyres took away the horse and cart. Bailey saw him and asked what he was doing. He said he was going to take the cart up the street as he did not know where Soffe was. Bailey, with some difficulty, got it into his stable and waited up to 12.30 for Soffe to collect it.

'Eyres and Kemish were drinking in the Bridge Tavern between 6 and 7 when they left together. Leach passed the Dolphin at 6 and said she had an old bloke in tow all day and was going back to him again as soon as Mary Sims had put her child to bed. Between 6 and 7 voices were heard going down the Causeway from the Bridge Tavern to Sadlers Mill. About this time a little boy Glasspool, son of a journeyman miller working at Sadlers Mill was standing near the Causeway. He heard voices coming from Pearce's Mead calling 'lay hold of the old B...' and two women screamed. Between 8 and 9

23

the 2 male prisoners were in the town drunk and enquiring for Leach, threatening if she did not dub up there would be a b….y row in the morning. The 2 men slept that night under a rick in the neighbourhood.

'Simes, being charged, said she left the Bridge Tavern at 6 with a Mrs Webb and went to her mother's house in Hog Lane and remained until 10 o'clock. She called Mrs Baratt, living next door, to prove it.

'All four were charged with wilful murder and ordered to take trial at the next assizes.'

NOTE: 'Baileys' probably relates to Charles Bailey of the *Blacksmiths Arms*.

*William IV sign*
*showing the bracket on which the cover design was based*

### The Romsey Advertiser of 10th March 1905:

An early-20th-century newspaper report that appeared in *The Romsey Advertiser* of 10th March 1905 evokes a colourful word-picture of that later era – and shows that drunken behaviour was not exclusively male, at least not in the rural districts surrounding Romsey.

'Mary Anne Barnes pleaded not guilty to a charge of being drunk in licensed premises at Copythorne. Evidence was given by P.S. Walsh and P.C. Kemp, and defendant said she had had a lot of worry since her husband's death. Fined 5s 0d and 5s 0d costs.

'Matilda Spratt of Cadnam was summoned for being drunk upon the highway. Defendant denied the drunkenness, saying she was only helpless. P.C. Spreadbury said he found the defendant lying helplessly drunk in a ditch. With assistance he got her out and as she could not walk he took her home.

'Defendant said she suffered from acute rheumatism in her knees, but had only had three-penny-worth of gin all day. A fine of 1s 0d and 6s. 6d. costs was imposed.'

The main roads in the Romsey area showing the outlying pubs

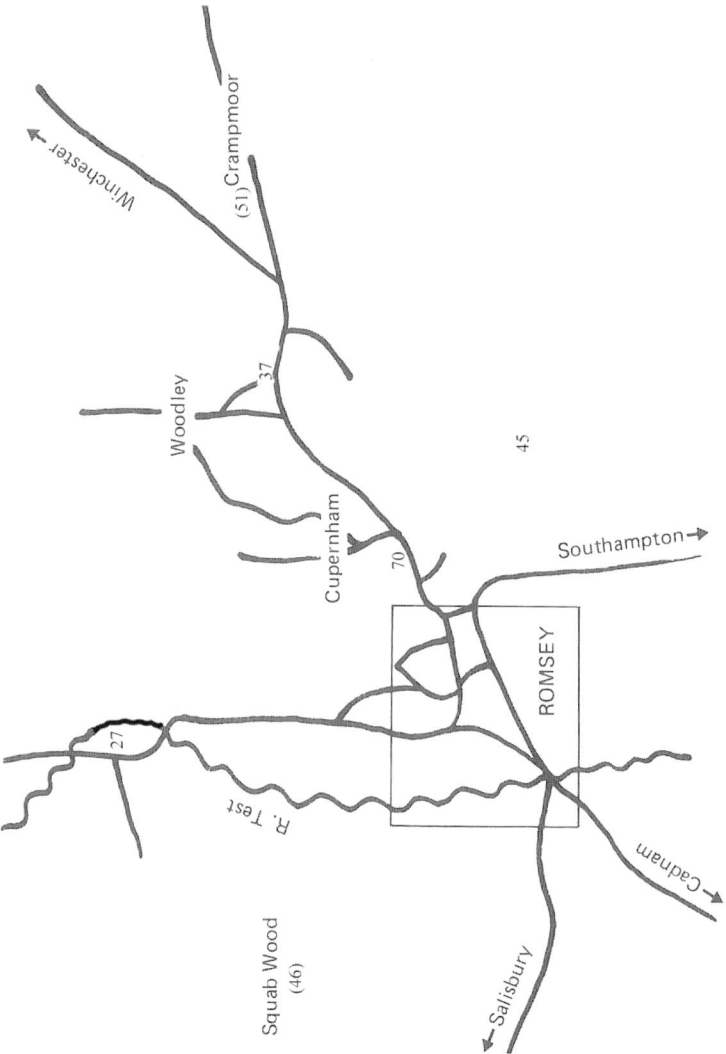

*Map of Outer Romsey*

The numbers refer to the pub numbers used in the text

Numbers for known locations under latest name
Numbers in brackets indicate uncertain locations

*Map of Inner Romsey*

26

# THE PUBS

This section features an alphabetical tour of the historic inns, pubs and ale-houses of Romsey with known history to date.

- ** denotes pubs that had already closed by 1974
- * denotes pubs that have closed since 1974
- ( ) show that this name is an earlier name for the pub described

## 1    Abbey Hotel, 11 Church Street
*(see also the Falcon and the Market Inn)*

Although the current *Abbey Hotel* is a new building by Romsey pub standards, it is in fact on the site of a much older inn, known in the 18<sup>th</sup> century and early 19<sup>th</sup> century as the *Falcon* and then as the *Market Inn*. The subsequent change to the *Abbey Hotel* came after the rebuilding of the 1890s, during the tenure of John Scorey. This rebuilding was the final part of a road-widening scheme in Church Street between the Market Place and Church Place. Most of the widening – which took the form of moving back the east side of the street – happened in the late 1870s, but there was a delay over the *Abbey Hotel* site because of a curious ownership situation. The north section was freehold but the south had long been leased from Winchester College. (As a charity, the College was restricted in respect of selling its property until the law was altered in the Victorian era.)

*Abbey Hotel, Church Street*

An interesting feature is the right of way over the driveway held by the property to the north (No 13 Church Street), which actually has a side door opening onto the hotel's drive. This right of way can be traced to the early 1800s, beyond which there are no helpful documents available. It is likely that the right has existed for centuries; it permits the passage of dung carts

27

and similar antiquated equipment. In the 21$^{st}$ century, its main use is the rather more mundane one of pushing 'wheelie bins' into position for weekly collections.

The *Abbey Hotel* was sold in 1915, and the sales particulars describe the attractions for potential buyers. On production of those sales particulars, the occupier of the time, Mr E.D. Jefford, was prepared to permit intending purchasers to view a property with a 54ft frontage that was 'most centrally situate in the old and thriving Market Town of Romsey, immediately opposite the fine Norman Abbey of SS Mary & Ethelfleda, with all its Historic Associations, and consequently of great attraction and interest to Travellers'.

After passing through the hotel entrance, prospective purchasers would see the coffee and dining rooms with a moveable partition making one room, averaging 28ft x 14ft, well-lighted by four windows, and fitted with two grates and a serving hatch. Good public and private bars, about 23ft x 19ft 6in, featured a register grate, and as added customer facilities there were a lavatory, WC and wine cellar.

Upstairs was a 'capital' billiard room (about 24ft x 19ft) with span ceiling light and two grates. Nearby were six good bedrooms each with a grate and iron mantel, and one small bedroom. The hotel also provided guests with a bathroom, with fixed bath and grate, a separate WC and a cloak cupboard on the landing.

The innkeeper could enjoy a generous private sitting room, 20ft x 12ft 6in, with a tiled grate, polished mantel, glass cupboard and two windows. There was an 'excellent kitchen' with oven and roaster range, dresser and china and glass cupboard. There were also a separate larder and a scullery equipped with a long wash-up trough, sink and washing copper.

The carriage entrance from the street led to 'an excellent enclosed yard' with brick and tiled stabling for nine horses with loft over, and modern stabling of four stalls and two loose boxes with iron mangers and racks. There was a separate harness room with grate. As a nod to new technology, it was pointed out that two lock-ups by the coach-house and other sheds could be easily converted into a garage. Beyond the outhouses was a large kitchen garden abutting the Holbrook stream.

By 1974, the premises had extended over the two adjoining shops, and offered fourteen bedrooms. Stone cellars suggested that the building was raised on much older foundations. Before relaxation of pub opening times, the *Abbey Hotel*, like certain other pubs in Romsey, could stay open a further hour until 3pm on Thursdays, the day of Romsey Market from 1826 until it ceased to operate as a weekly cattle market in the 1960s.

For some years during the second half of the 20$^{th}$ century, the *Abbey Hotel* bore a sign depicting a monk, a rather unfortunate illustration for an inn that took its name from the nearby Abbey church of a one-time Benedictine nunnery.

## 2    Angel Hotel, 21 Bell Street *

The *Angel* appeared in the oldest available directory, that of 1784, when Richard Garrett was the licensee. By 1792 he had been replaced by William Chalk. Most of the early licensees described themselves as beer retailers only. It is not clear from the records when the house gained a full licence. However, the house seems to have prospered.

The present building dates from the beginning of the 19th century, replacing an earlier one that burned down in 1800, and there are clues to the existence of an earlier building on a similar lay-out. These clues lie in the considerable depth of the building, and in the presence of medieval cellars under the present structure. The use - or successive uses - of the premises prior to the 18th century is uncertain.

*The Angel Hotel building, Bell Street*

The *Angel* was advertised in directories all through the 19th century, and its Victorian appearance was enhanced by decorative glass and stucco décor. Unfortunately, the *Angel* did not enjoy a very good reputation in the 19th century. In 1827, a constable, Thomas Butt, was assaulted when he attempted to quell a serious riot there. Four young men were arrested and brought up at the next town sessions.

Then, in the mid-1800s, when the innkeeper was a Mr Floyd, the *Angel* really became the focus of low life in Romsey. Mr Floyd had transferred from the *Globe* in Mill Lane, and seems to have been a free-drinking irresponsible publican, who allowed his wife to run what was virtually a bawdy house. Mrs Floyd encouraged use of her six or seven bedrooms for many illicit relationships. Some of the women had already been 'clients' or servants at the *Globe*.

Ellizabeth Goddard, who worked for the Floyds, later gave evidence against them in an undated affidavit witnessed by Charles Tylee, a partner in a Portersbridge Street legal practice. The affidavit detailed some of the unsavoury activities of a group of young women and an assortment of men, and Elizabeth admitted 'I never saw any respectable persons come to the house in my life – I know Mrs Floyd keeps a very bad house …'. She signed her declaration with a cross. It was either at the *Angel*, or earlier at the *Globe*, that Elizabeth had witnessed some of the debauchery through a hole in the floorboards.

More prosaic information about this building in the late 19th-century comes from the sale of The Horsefair Brewery in 1875, when the *Angel* was one of

29

its tied pubs, worth £12 a year in rent inclusive of ancillary properties (a right of way being separately valued at 2s per annum).

~~~~~~~~

### CAPITAL FREEHOLD PUBLIC-HOUSE
### Known as 'THE ANGEL"
With Butcher's Shop and Dwelling-House adjoining

Situate in Bell Street, Romsey, both newly-erected and substantially built of brick. The Public-house contains Bar, Parlour, Tap-room, Kitchen, four Bedrooms, Yard, 5-stall Stable, Cart-house, Cow-house, Wash-house, Stable and Loft, Small Garden, and is in the occupation of Mrs Mabbit.

The House and Shop are in the occupation of Mr Webb, and include – Stabling for two horses, brick-built Slaughter-house and large Yard, and other conveniences, with gateway entrance to Newton Lane.

The right of way, about 26ft wide, on the north side of the above Inn and Shop, is included in the sale.

~~~~~~~~

The Webbs mentioned in this sales notice had a long association with the *Angel*, partly because a Joseph Webb was licensee in 1852 and partly because of their butcher's shop. This was situated at the front of the building at the southern end. The shop had its own front door onto the street. Later, Eastmans took over the butcher's shop and ran it into the early 20th century. Meathooks from this era survived in a storage area.

Generally, the actual licensees of the *Angel* did not appear to carry on a second trade, although Richard Garrett hired out a post chaise. Thomas Mills in 1878 called himself a victualler and in 1898 he was advertising 'good stabling, horses and carriage for hire, rendezvous for cyclists'.

The *Angel* was one of the pubs that benefited from the weekly market, and was allowed to open later on Thursday afternoons. In the 20th century the market was held behind the *Angel*. One Romsonian in the 1970s remembered being tied to the cart as a small child while her father and grandfather availed themselves of refreshment at the *Angel*.

In the final decades of the 20th century, perhaps due to the closure of the Newton Lane market, the *Angel* faltered, stopped being a pub and was transformed into a popular restaurant, *La Parisienne*.

*La Parisienne*

# 3    Barley Mow, 103-107 The Hundred **
*(see also the Wheatsheaf, the Cartwheel and the Packhorse)*

The *Barley Mow* used to be in The
Hundred, where Alma Terrace now
stands between the entrance to the
Harrage and the Police Station.  The
name first appears in a mortgage
indenture of 1823, when the pub is
described as 'all that messuage,
tenement or public house lately called
the *Cartwheel* but then called the
*Barley Mow*'.

*Alma Terrace, built on site of the Barley Mow*

It is likely that the change of name followed the change of ownership that
had occurred a couple of years earlier.  This pub was one of those owned by
the brewer, John Latham, at the time of his bankruptcy in 1817.   His
properties were sold off by the bankruptcy assignees over the next couple of
years.    Several of the Latham pubs seem to have been renamed
subsequently, as new owners sought to distance themselves from the
bankruptcy scandal, especially after John Latham shot himself in 1822.

The house was a coaching inn.  When entering, it was necessary to drive
around the duck pond (now covered by the Police Station) and enter from
the south.   When John Latham bought the property from John Fleming in
1795 he paid £525 for it, but this value had almost halved by the mid-19th
century, probably as the coaching trade diminished or perhaps because the
site had already been reduced in size.

In 1851 Elizabeth Miller, aged 51, lived there with her son as a house
servant and a lodger, Ann Tuck.  The Craven & Co. trade directory of 1857
named Elizabeth Cole as victualler.  Perhaps Mrs Miller remarried, but there
is further confusion about this period when for a time the house was known
as the *Packhorse*.  A deed of 1841 describes 'all that messuage or public
house known as *The Packhorse*, then lately called *The Barley Mow* and
formerly called *The Cartwheel*, formerly in the occupation of Charles
Waterman then of James Cook and now or late of the tenure or occupation
of Joseph Meby'.  By 1859, the description had partly reversed the sequence
of the names, referring to 'all that messuage or public house known as *The
Barley Mow*, lately called *The Packhorse*, formerly *The Cartwheel*, then in the
occupation of Mrs Cole'.   It is virtually impossible to match all these
occupiers with the pub name for their time in the premises.

It seems, however, that the pub reverted to the *Barley Mow* name towards
the end of its existence.  Sales particulars for the premises under the name
of the *Barley Mow* were issued in 1858, when the frontage was given as 70
feet.  The pub was demolished prior to Alma Terrace being built on the site
in 1869.

31

## 4 Bell Inn, 32 Bell Street **

This was one of the Romsey public houses that catered for well-to-do travellers of the turnpike era. It was claimed that the Prince Regent once changed horses there, and its continued prosperity is reflected in the grand 19th-century frontage to the street. The inn, however, had existed for much longer than its façade might suggest, and was already well-established in the 17th century.

John Hacke, innkeeper of the *Bell Inn*, died in 1687 worth £72 5s 6d, a good sum for the time. His inventory invokes a splendid word picture of the inn in his day. The principal rooms were rather grandly referred to as the Parlour, the Bell Chamber, the Hall Chamber and the Crown Chamber. Despite these impressive names, however, most of these rooms contained only basic furniture, much of it referred to as 'old'. The usual bedsteads, truckle beds, cupboards, table boards, chests, coffers, bed linen and hangings, and fire irons are listed. The most expensive furniture was assembled in the Crown Chamber, where there were a dozen leather chairs worth £2 2s 0d; good quality bed curtains and window curtains; feather and flock beds, bolsters and pillows; carpet and rugs. Together with fire tongs and other small items the contents of the Crown Chamber were worth about £15 in total.

More prosaically, there were also a kitchen, a hall, a brewhouse, a cellar and a 'chamber over the cellar'. The most valuable items in the kitchen were the pewter dishes, worth £4 8s 1d. The brass pots were valued at £2 2s 8d. Like the pewter, they were appraised by weight as were also the old banded kettles and iron goods, worth 17s 8d and 14s 0d respectively.

Household linen – sheets, table cloths, napkins, pillow ties, towels – were assessed at £3 16s 7d. About 'a tunn of ale' in the brewhouse was worth £3 10s 0d, but the six hogheads, six half hogheads and one firkin, three stands and 6 dozen bottles were only worth £2 16s 0d in total. In the back yard, or 'backside', there was a clutter of 400 faggots for the fire, 12 loads of dung and a hay rick, along with other odds and ends.

John Hacke's widow, Joan, carried on the business for a while, and after her came Stephen Spragg. The next recorded licensee was John Coles, in whose day the inn was seemingly known as 'the *Blew Bell*'. Evidence for this is found in a document of 1731, which refers to
> '... all that messuage tenement and garden ... heretofore in the occupation of Stephen Spragg and late in the occupation of Joan Hack Widow and then and now in the occupation of John Coles commonly called or known by the name of the *Blew Bell Inn* ....'

Not only was the inn's name rather different but its location was given as Mill Street. It was only later in the 18th century that the inn gave its own name to the street, previously called after the Town Mill just to the south of the inn.

At the Romsey Court Leet meeting held on 31<sup>st</sup> October 1771, the following order was one of several made:

> We also present that the sign post of the *Bell Inn* is a nuisance and that the same ought to be removed viz. in case Mr Stephen Hornshead the present owner of the said *Bell Inn* do not remove the said signpost in one month from this time we amerce him the sum of forty shillings.

Making an order and enforcing it were two very different matters. Repetitions of orders against various erring townspeople appear all too regularly in the court records. In the case of the *Bell Inn*, a report in 1784 suggests that Mr Hornshead had either ignored instructions or had replaced the offending sign with one presenting similar difficulties. In that year, M. Jean Pierre Blanchard, the balloonist, landed in Romsey on a flight from London. The balloon was brought into town, but could not proceed up Bell Street because of the narrowness of the street and especially because of the obstruction caused by the *Bell Inn* sign. The balloon had to be taken down Banning Street and across a field and thence up The Hundred.

The inn had a long history of association with the transport industry. In the 18<sup>th</sup> century, John Faithorne was advertising a post chaise for hire. During Thomas Travers' time there in the 1830s, the Gosport coach arrived from Bristol each day at 5pm and Webb's Stage Waggons called every Tuesday, Thursday and Saturday.

However, it is interesting to note how few people lived there in 1851. According to the census of that year, James Rigg, aged fifty, his wife, three children, an ostler, and a lodger were the sole inhabitants. In the 1850s, James Rigg was advertising the services of local carriers. On Thursdays, Mills went to Bramshaw, and, on Tuesdays and Saturdays, Noble went to Plaitford and Wellow. The place was also a posting house, keeping changes of horse for coaches travelling a long distance.

Mrs Martha Mary Rigg died in 1857, and in 1859 the property ceased to be a hostelry.

*The old Bell Inn*

The *Bell Inn* was still closed in 1875 when it was sold as an asset of The Horsefair Brewery. In the sales particulars it was said to bring in an annual rent of £15. More fully, it was described as:

A CAPITAL FREEHOLD COMMERCIAL HOTEL
Known as 'THE BELL'
Situate in Bell Street, in the town of Romsey, recently entirely renovated and put in thorough order by the lessee at a large cost, and containing – *On the Ground floor* – Bar, Parlour, Coffee-room, Market-room, Kitchen, Scullery, &c.; Tap at side of house and three rooms. *Upper floor* – seven bedrooms & six Attics. Good Cellarage. *In the rear* – Coach-house, two 6-stall Stables, Stable for 12 horses, Open Shed, W.C.
At present unoccupied

~~~~~~~

This description suggests that there had been hopes of revitalising the *Bell Inn* as a pub, but this was not to be. A handwritten annotation to the sales particulars indicate that the erstwhile inn was sold on for £800.

The property was eventually acquired as business premises by Mr Roles, a builder and plumber. Indeed, there was a restrictive clause in the contract that the house might not be used as a licensed house ever again. Ironically, it was transport that forced the closure of the *Bell Inn*, a staging post that could no longer retain its viability once the new-fangled rail network had undermined the coaching trade that had formerly sustained Romsey's major inns. Only those that had diversified managed to survive.

A successful trade premises in the late-19th and early-20th century, the *Bell Inn* was unused for some years, then renovated and advertised as offices in the early 1970s. This was a far cry from its earlier peaks of success, such as when John Hack, as the proprietor, was issuing his own ½d trade tokens in 1667, and had a separate 'garden' further west at the far side of the present Newton Lane carpark.

# 5 Bellringers Arms, possibly Cherville Street **

This is one of the ethereal houses that is hard to trace. It is mentioned in a private scrapbook as existing in 1854. Further endorsement of its existence came from Mr Stephen Ward, a road carrier for rail freight until the 1960s. He wrote a letter stating that he believed the pub to have been opposite the *Vine*, in which case the building used has probably been pulled down. There seems to be no firm documentary evidence for the *Bellringers Arms*, although there is a strong verbal tradition to support its existence.

# 6 Bishop Blaize, 4 Winchester Road

By Romsey standards, this is a middle-aged pub, since it appears to date from the 18th century. The name of the road in which it stands has varied between The Hundred, Winchester Street and Winchester Road. Despite that, the building seems to have looked the same for many years: in 1859, the Pavement Commissioners referred to the long space in front of the *Bishop Blaize*, a feature that survives.

The name of the *Bishop Blaize* is a reminder of Romsey's association with the wool trade. St Blaize was the patron saint of woolcombers. In 1530 a light was burned to the Bishop in St Laurence's, the parish church, which was then restricted to the north aisle and transept of the Abbey church. (The town did not have use of the entire church building until after the dissolution of the Benedictine nunnery in 1539; before then the nuns had possession of the major part.) The present house was built in 1708 when Romsey's wool trade was very old, so there could have been an earlier *Bishop Blaize*.

At the latter end of the 18th century, John Jones was the licensee. Nearly 200 years later, a ½d dated 1760 was found on the premises. Had it once belonged to this man, or perhaps to a customer?

*The Bishop Blaize, Winchester Road*

There is no cellar, nor any evidence of brewing. The house may well have been tied for a very long time. Licensees are recorded throughout the 19th century, although there is confusion regarding 1859. Thomas Higgins, Thomas Higgs and Mrs Jane Turner are all shown as licensees. The most reliable source gives Higgs, so Higgins is probably a mistake; Mrs Turner is a mystery, unless she took over the licence during the year.

In the 1970s, the building still had numbers on its bar doors, these being a relic of times when the individual rooms were licensed. Since then the small rooms have been opened up to make a more open bar. Not only the numbers but many of the doors have disappeared.

Until the mid-20th century, there was another building between the Bishop Blaize and the corner of Alma Road, but this was demolished when Alma Road was widened.

## 7  Blacksmiths Arms, Middlebridge Street **

The *Blacksmiths Arms* stood on the south side of Middlebridge Street, close to the bridge.  Along with other nearby properties – including the original Bartlett's Almshouses - it was pulled down in the 1930s to make way for the by-pass.  The name of this pub must surely be linked to its occupation at one stage by a Mr Tutt, who was both a retailer of beer and a blacksmith.  Mr Mansbridge was another blacksmith who held the licence there.   Its location on the edge of town would have been good for both trades, catching travellers as they left Romsey with little prospect of similar services for some miles to come, though its drinking facilities would have had little appeal to wealthier folk.

*Blacksmiths Arms, 1904*

The earliest known reference to the *Blacksmiths Arms* relates to a mortgage deed of 1822.  In this, the owners – Figes & Longcroft the brewers – were citing the *Blacksmiths Arms* as one of the pubs on which the mortgage was being raised.  The most obvious clue to the existence of this pub, however, was found in the form of a photograph, taken in 1905 and inscribed '*The Blacksmiths Arms*'.  The photograph shows no signboard outside to indicate its use as a pub, but, subsequently, in the 1970s, two or three older Romsonians said they thought it was a pub until after the First World War.

The best documentary evidence is found in an inventory made on the 29th May 1855, when Charles Baily seems to have put up all his worldly goods as security for a loan agreement.  It is pretty certain that Charles Baily was the brewer cum grocer cum baker who ran the *Blacksmiths Arms*.  The 1851 Census gives Charles Bailey, a baker and brewer aged 39 years, living with his wife and three young children in a Middlebridge Street property listed immediately after the Palmerston Lodge – the right location for the *Blacksmiths Arms*.  The fact that the loan was made by Alfred Pitt Jesser and Francis Cressey, who ran the Jesser and Cressey brewery, gives further support, and so do the contents of the inventory.

36

The inventory gives full details about the property, about the typical contents of a mid-19<sup>th</sup>-century home and about the life-style of the man himself. It indicates that Charles Baily pursued several activities, though presumably none of them very profitably since he was desperate for additional funds. And although the *Blacksmiths Arms* gives a certain authority to Baily's role as mine host, it appears that his bakery business may have been more significant - the 1851 Census also records his younger brother and sister living in as baker's assistants. Charles and his brother and sister, incidentally, all came from the village of Ampfield on the Romsey-Winchester road; his wife, Mary, from Hursley just beyond Ampfield.

The building itself, according to the inventory, consisted of a shop, a tap room where beer would be served, a kitchen, a sitting room and three bedrooms upstairs. Underneath was a cellar. The outbuildings included a bakehouse, a storehouse, a brewhouse, a stable, and a smoke-loft. Somewhere amongst them there was a yard. Charles Baily also had a small holding in Waldron Lane to the south, where there were stables, a carthouse, a slaughterhouse and other such buildings.

It can be deduced that he grew wheat, had at some point kept and slaughtered pigs, and owned at least one horse. He baked bread and presumably sold it in the shop, but, as he no longer seemed to have any pigs, perhaps he no longer sold home-smoked ham and other pig products, though he still had all the apparatus to prepare them. Similarly, he may or may not have still used the brewhouse to brew his own ale. The financial links with local breweries suggest that the pub's supplies came from them.

The state of the shop may have been normal in the mid-Victorian era, but the unhealthy sounding jumble may represent a lack of industry that led to financial need. Inside there were two shop counters with drawers, a separate nest of 19 drawers and three tables. There was also a desk where presumably Charles Baily wrote out his bills and kept his accounts. There were shelves all round the shop. Some would have been occupied by the goods for sale, but there were other things on the shelves or on the tables and counters. There was a tobacco jar and box plus 3 scales and an assortment of weights from 56lbs downwards. On the floor was a double flour bin and two offal bins, each with three partitions. In a corner were eighteen bushel bags and a pair of hand-trucks. On a dark winter evening it would be proudly lit by the two gas burners that had been fitted. A collection of liquid measures in both pewter and earthenware, together with funnels, tumblers and ale glasses hint at an overlap between the shop and the nearby tap room.

The tap room was where the locals came to be served their favourite brew. Here there were three large deal tables. There was little scope for rearranging the furniture as the seats were fixed all round the room with just two free-standing stools available. One solitary gas burner illuminated the scene. There was no mention of oil lamps and candles but presumably they would have been available.

The kitchen was furnished with a deal table, an oak leaf table and six Windsor chairs. Perhaps the two cupboards mentioned filled the recesses either side of the fireplace, which had a basket grate and a set of fire-irons. Three 'Cocoa Nut' mats protected the floor, while ten various brushes were available to keep the house in order. Four trays were useful for carrying the tea set and other crockery, and sundry knives and forks.

An attempt had been made to make the sitting room cosy with a drugget and a hearth rug in front of the fender, behind which was another set of fire-irons and a copper coal scuttle. On the mantelpiece were ten chimney ornaments. A mahogany two-flap dining table was surrounded by 6 cane-seated chairs, one of them with arms. There was a pair of metal candlesticks to set out on the table. Against the wall was a tea table with the fashionable tea caddy on it and the better tea ware. The lady of the house might have her two work boxes nearby as she sat down for a while. A rolling blind at the window perhaps protected against strong sunlight. And there were a few books, too, as well as a revolver pistol and case.

Going up the stairs to the bedrooms led past the 24-hour clock in its oak case. The first bedroom sounds charming - fresh and cosy. There was a tent bedstead with a choice of two white counterpanes or one coloured one. There was a flock mattress and a feather bed as well as a bolster and two pillows, with the option of 13 blankets and 6 pairs of sheets. Dimity furniture meant that the hangings of the bed were of dimity material - a stout cotton with raised stripes or pattern. A painted washstand had blue and white ware on it. An oak chest of drawers was perhaps a good place for the mahogany framed looking glasses. Two large clothes chests also helped to keep the bedroom tidy, and a degree of comfort was implied by 3 cane-seated chairs, a bedside carpet and a brass fender, which of course indicates a fire. The most evocative item was a child's crib.

The other two bedrooms also sound pleasant if a little more stark. The second one had an oak four-poster bed, again with flock mattress, feather bed, bolster and two pillows. This time the hangings were chintz. There was a bedside carpet and the fender was a painted one. The furniture consisted simply of a painted dressing table and three cane-seated chairs.

In the final bedroom another tent bedstead was hung with white dimity and provided with a feather bed, a bolster and a pillow. Two rush-seated chairs and a looking glass seem to have been the only furniture, but all the bedrooms may have had built-in cupboards, which would not be listed. Somewhere was stored the linen collection of four tablecloths and eleven assorted towels.

In the cellar was a large meat-silt lined with lead, a salting tub and also a meat safe, perhaps originally related to the pig rearing. In connection with the pub side of Baily's business there were three barrel stands, one small mash tub and eight small casks.

38

Outside, the bake-house was ready for action. There was a kneading trough, a moulding bench and two oven peals or shovels, one made of iron and one of wood. There were scales, weights and baking tins, a fixed 12-gallon cast-iron boiler, a 4-gallon iron pot and two lard beaters, all representative of hard work. In a store room there was a mill fixed on the floor and a pair of hand trucks

The brew-house was dominated by the 100-gallon fixed copper, but there was also a mash tub, a fixed malt mill, pumps and pipes, coolers and tubs. Two pairs of steps were ready for any use. It should be noted that there was a link between brewing and baking with bakers sometimes doubling up as maltsters.

The stable housed the only four-legged animal mentioned in the inventory. This was a gray horse, but it sounded as if there had been more at some time, judging by the amount of harness and other equipment. There were three leather head stalls, halters and clogs, two pairs of plough harness and traces, and other harness such as brass-mounted gig harness, besides six horse collars and brushes and combs. A prong and shovel and two sieves completed the picture here.

A smoke loft was practically empty. The 16 iron crooks, all that was in the smoke loft, must have been hooks for hanging meat during the smoke-curing process.

Outside, the yard contained much evidence of pig-rearing, but there was no mention at all of the live animal. 20 feet of cast iron pig troughs, a fixed oak hog chest, hog pails and two pig-killing stools all suggest that quite a few animals were kept on the premises at some time. The yard was further cluttered by a wagon, two carts, two wheel barrows, plough, assorted buckets, two ladders and, living a somewhat hazardous existence, 16 fowl.

Charles Baily's small holding was in Waldron Lane, within the present Broadlands estate. There he had a slaughter house, three pig sties and two swinging chests, as well as numerous other outbuildings. These included a slated shed, two stables - one being brick built and slated - a carthouse and a barn, all with the sorts of apparatus associated with such places. Again, though, there was no mention of any pigs in the piggery. Either this activity had been abandoned or the inventory had already reached an acceptable value against the loan without them being included.

One of the two stables held mangers and stall partitions; the other – brick built and slated – had stall, coops, mangers, rack and loft, corn bin, chaff cutting box and knife. There were more mangers in the carthouse, and a winnowing machine in the barn. He was growing wheat in both the Hop Gardens and Middle Field, making 14½ acres in total.

All Charles Baily's possessions, as listed in the inventory, were committed to secure a loan of £91 18s 6d. They represent the life-style not only of

39

Charles Baily but of many similar licensees who had to mix victualling with other activities in order to make any sort of living.

Later Mr Holloway from the *Woolpack* ran his dairy from the *Blacksmiths Arms'* building. The building ended its days as a common lodging house, by which time it was in a very fragile state. On one occasion the passing of a steam wagon caused the collapse of an inside wall, and on another a child went through a floorboard when jumping about. It is questionable as to whether all the rooms were habitable by then.

## 8 (Black Swan)
*(see the Swan & Dolphin and the Star)*

The *Black Swan* may have been a one-time name for the *Star* in the Horsefair. Certainly, until the early 1800s, the *Star* was known in the records as the *Swan and Dolphin,* thus offering a splendid opportunity for confusion with both the *Swan* in the Market Place and the *Dolphin* in the Cornmarket. Calling it the *Black Swan* would have at least distinguished it from the (*White*) *Swan* in the Market Place, besides avoiding any reference to the *Dolphin*.

No mention of the 'Black Swan' has been found subsequent to 1800. This would be compatible with the pub's renaming as the *Star*, following the 1817 collapse of the Latham Brewery, which had owned the premises as the *Swan and Dolphin*.

## 9 Bricklayers Arms, Banning Street **
*(see the Fleur de Lis/Flower de Luce)*

The *Bricklayers Arms* was formerly the *Fleur de Lis* or *Flower de Luce*, and occasional references to this earlier name are found between 1784 and 1823. The building itself may be older, perhaps as much as three hundred years old. Although the frontage of this one-time pub suggests a smallish establishment, it is, in fact, quite substantial. The downstairs windows are interesting, since they are sash windows that open by sliding sideways.

By 1830, the pub was appearing in Pigot's Directory as the *Bricklayers Arms*. It may have acquired its link with the brick industry from the Floyd family, the male members of which established a local dynasty of bricklayers in the mid-18th century. The Floyds dominated the bricklaying scene in Romsey for about a hundred years, and much of their building activity was centred around Banning Street. They developed large sites along the one-time medieval thoroughfare, creating the courts and alley-ways that would become chronically overcrowded in later decades.

One of the exceptions to the bricklaying tradition was Henry Floyd, who very appropriately was the 1830 innholder at the *Bricklayers Arms*. An earlier Floyd, John, had also been an innholder in 1781, but his location is not given.

In the 1840s, there was a Wesleyan Methodist Chapel at the end of Banning Street, which must have had a certain status, as the Gas Company thought it worthwhile to extend the gas main to it. The ladies of the Chapel, however, became unhappy with the locality and the taunts received from the local lads. Perhaps those tormentors congregated at the *Bricklayers Arms*, which was next to the Chapel. Perhaps, too, the pub was a focal point for the self-styled Skeleton Army, an *ad hoc* rabble that aimed to demoralise the more robust Salvation Army folk who took over the Chapel building when the Methodists left.

From the mid-19th century until the early 20th century, the *Bricklayers Arms* was run by successive members of the Edwards family, related to the Edwards who ran the *Dolphin*. Business must have slumped during the First World War, when a huge number of young men from the local vicinity went into the army.

*The old Bricklayers Arms, Banning Street
with new properties being built at rear in 2005*

Jess Edwards, the last of the Edwards at the *Bricklayers Arms*, was succeeded by Mr and Mrs Spencer, and after them the licensees were Mr and Mrs Jack Jones. In 1962, the Jones were succeeded by their niece and her husband, Mr and Mrs Barlow. Mrs Barlow claimed to remember regular fights in the street, although she never had any trouble in the pub herself. The Barlows were the last licensees. Although the building survived, the pub ceased to operate in the mid-20th century, when all the little cottages were swept away to make room for Council flats, and Banning Street was severely truncated.

The *Bricklayers Arms* seems to have given steady service without fuss over the centuries. It must have mainly served the locals since Banning Street had gradually dwindled into a mere side street in the post-medieval period.

In 2005, the property was undergoing renovation with new dwellings being erected at the rear of the site.

41

## 10 Bridge Tavern, 1 Mainstone **
*(see The White Hart)*

For a long time Middlebridge Street continued over the bridge into Mainstone and as far as the foot of Pauncefoot Hill. The address for this property has therefore fluctuated. But the situation of the *Bridge Tavern* was quite good for catching travellers from the west, and for attracting locals from the southern part of Romsey. For travellers from the west, it was the last property before crossing Middlebridge and entering Romsey Infra with its more stringent drinking controls. For locals of lower Middlebridge Street, it was the first available pub outside the controls of Romsey Infra. The population was growing, and many new pubs were opening, and it was a tempting location for a pub, especially once the turnpike roads had evolved in the mid-18th century. But the site was limited by the lack of a side entrance for vehicles, a fact that became increasingly significant over time.

Initially, this pub operated under the name of the *White Hart*, for which there are occasional records between 1784 and 1830. In its later time as the *Bridge Tavern*, the pub only had a short 60-year history stretching from c1850 to 1911, when it closed. In its final years, at least, the *Bridge* was only a modest beer-house.

*The old Bridge Tavern*

There is a nice overlap in the change from the *White Hart* to the *Bridge Tavern*, when John Young appeared as licensee under both pub names. This was at a time when the pub names seem to have overlapped in the records.

Confirmation of the link between the two names appears in the 1875 sales particulars for The Horsefair Brewery, owner of the *Bridge Tavern* at that time.

~~~~~~

A FREEHOLD BEER-HOUSE

Known as 'THE BRIDGE' (formerly known as 'THE WHITE HART')

Close to the above *[meaning 'The Lamb']*, and containing four rooms on Ground floor, four ditto above. Kitchen, Cellar, &c., on basement. Yard and 3-stall Stable. In the occupation of Mr Young.

~~~~~~

An early mention of the *Bridge Tavern* is found for 1854: it does not reflect well on the establishment at that time. John Chandler of the *Bridge Tavern* was fined £5 and costs for opening his house at half past twelve on Sunday, 20 August. Thereafter, the pub was in the hands of the Young family for many years. John Young was there in the 1850s and Mrs Matilda Young in the 1870s and 1880: by 1885 another John Young was in control. The Young family may not have been so lax on time-keeping and may have run it more successfully. Nevertheless, the *Bridge Tavern*'s rental value of £5 in 1875 compares poorly with its neighbouring pubs, the *Lamb* to the west at £9 10s 0d and the *Three Tuns* to the east at no less than £30 (although that included the two adjacent cottages). Indeed, the *Bridge Tavern* carried the lowest valuation of all the Romsey pubs then owned by The Horsefair Brewery.

In the 1970s, Mr Ward - long-term rail freight carrier of the Old Manor House in Palmerston Street - could remember a man named Tongs doing wickerwork there, but did not give a date. The place lost its licence in the purge of 1911 when it was pointed out that there was no pull-in for vehicles and the tenant had other work besides his licence. Strong's, the owners, received £468 compensation and James Stott, the licensee, £35.

# 11 (Bugle, 3, Cornmarket)
(see The Tudor Rose)

In the 1970s, older Romsonians remembered the jingle:
> Up and down the Market Place
> In and out the Bugle
> That's the way the money goes
> Pop goes the weasel

The *Bugle* referred to was in The Cornmarket, and it had been a pub since at least the 19th century. As a modest beer house, it presumably once sold home-brewed beer, for deeds of 1834 refer to a brewhouse on the premises.

The earliest known owners of the property were members of the Footner family. Although the Footners emerged in the 19th century as local solicitors and bankers, a William Footner was recorded in 1797 as a wine merchant and maltster. This would link in well with a brew-house on the premises. There are, however, no known licensees before Mrs Sarah Cole in 1871.

At the end of the 19th or beginning of the 20th century the licensee, John Barfield, supplemented his income by selling beef. He obtained flank beef by hamper from London. He then sold it under the archway of the carriage entrance for 4d per lb every Thursday. Several of the tenants at the beginning of the 20th century were also bakers, and some of their implements survived.

*The Bugle, The Cornmarket, c1920s*

43

One old Romsonian, writing about his childhood in 1908, described how it was his job to go and fetch his father's beer. 'The bottles had screw tops and, before leaving, the landlord Mr Jim Dod would melt a little sealing wax, by means of a small gas jet and seal the cork to the bottle. Presumably that was the law in those days.'

In 1928, the *Bugle* was undergoing substantial renovations, which revealed it to be a very interesting 15th-century property. The pub was promptly renamed the *Tudor Rose*.


**SPECIAL NOTE**: *The following entries regarding the name Cartwheel or Cart Wheel have been distilled from a confusion of contradictory evidence. There were undoubtedly two establishments using the name, seemingly at much the same time. There was certainly one in The Hundred, but whether there were one or two in the south-west part of town is debatable.*

# 12 (Cartwheel, The Hundred **)
*(see the Barley Mow and the Packhorse)*

In 1974, LTVAS researchers had to weigh up conflicting claims for the precise location of the *Cartwheel* in The Hundred.

They had access to the work of Mrs Suckling of Highwood House (now Stroud School) who had been writing about Romsey and its local history in the early 20th century. She linked the *Cartwheel* with the *Catherine Wheel*, which in turn became the *Sawyers Arms* at No 95 The Hundred. She may have been encouraged by the name of Robert Carter, who appears in records as licensee of the *Catherine Wheel* in 1792 and 1798. He was also a licensee of the *Cartwheel*, but this could be an instance of one person obtaining more than one licence.

There were also claims that the *Cartwheel* was to be found further east on the site of present-day Alma Terrace. New documentary evidence has since endorsed this second alternative.

Alma Terrace was erected in 1869. House deeds recite that this Victorian terrace was built on the site of the *Barley Mow*, previously called the *Cartwheel*. Renaming may well have taken place quite soon after the Latham bankruptcy sales. Certainly, the purchasers of some of the disgraced brewer's other licensed premises seem to have made a fresh start with a new name. The *Cartwheel* had definitely become the *Barley Mow* by 1823, when an indenture of mortgage in respect of an Alma Terrace property described 'all that messuage tenement or public house lately called the *Cartwheel* but then called the *Barley Mow*'.

A detailed description of the *Cartwheel* in The Hundred has also been found since 1974. This pub was one of the group belonging to the brewer, John Latham, who had acquired it in 1795. It was sold following his bankruptcy in

1817, and a description in the sales particulars shows that it was quite a substantial enterprise. It reads as follows:

> Lot 5    The Cartwheel, The Hundred, Romsey
> A freehold public house, known by the sign of the *Cart Wheel*; containing four bedrooms, parlour, bar, and large tap room, with stabling for six horses; a large room adjoining, and other outhouses thereto belonging, and a large garden behind; situate in the Hundred of Romsey now in the occupation of Mr Waterman, at the yearly rent of £14 who holds the same, under an agreement to quit, on receiving three months notice.
> The House can, at a trifling expense, be rendered capable of carrying on a good beer and spirit trade, as it is situate in a very populous neighbourhood.

# 13 Cart Wheel, Newton Lane **

Yet another *Cartwheel* pub appears in the Land Tax records of 1800. These show that the brewer, John Latham, also owned this property with Nick Slade as his tenant. The rate of tax was 18s 4d, which was quite high, and indicates that the house must have been fairly substantial.

The Land Tax records give only a vague idea of the pub's exact location, but fortunately other more descriptive, though still imprecise, information has emerged. It comes in the form of an Abstract of Title – a certified legal document reciting the history of a property to assure any purchaser that the vendor had a legal right to sell. It was needed in respect of brewer John Latham's bankruptcy sales after his business collapsed in 1817.

This abstract states in the heading that the *Cartwheel* was in Middlebridge Street. This probably means the Middlebridge Street tithing (or ward) for the Abstract then proceeds to describe the pub's location in Newton Lane, as follows:

> *Reciting that* said John Latham was possessed of one other public house in Romsey aforesaid called the *Cart Wheel* then in the occupation of Thomas Purchase in a certain Lane there called Newton Lane nigh unto a Garden Plott then late Stephen Hammonds on the East Part An orchard of Thos Craddocks on the West part the Highway on the North part and an Orchard of Swithin Childs and said lane on the south part with a piece or parcel of land ground and meadow situate and being in Romsey aforesaid in said County of Southampton by virtue of a lease dated the 1st day of November 1792 granted by the Masters and Scholars Clerks of the College of St Mary in the City of Winchester to John Sanders of the town and County of Southampton Brewer for the term of 20 years under the yearly rent of 12/- and three bushels of wheat and two bushels and a half / payable as therein mentioned / and by him said John Sanders sold to said John Latham and conveyed by assignment dated the 21st day of December 1795.

And reciting that John Latham having occasion for the sum of £500 had applied to and requested said Richard Fifield to advance and lend him same ............ [with above property as surety].

*NOTE: This description, despite being very detailed, creates considerable confusion. Not only is it ambivalent about the pub's location – Middlebridge Street v. Newton Lane – but the references to 'the highway' on the north and 'said lane' on the south do not relate to the lay-out of that area in any way. This undermines the usefulness of the document.*

There is no later history for this pub to date. Perhaps it ceased to operate as a pub after the sale, or it may - like others from Latham's ownership – have received a new name. But no connection can be made with the only other definitely known pub in Newton Lane - the *Newton Arms* - which only entered the records in 1890.

## 14 (Cartwheel, Middlebridge Street/Mainstone **)
*(see the Horse and Jockey)*

The final possible location of a pub known as the *Cartwheel* is Mainstone, the small development beyond Middlebridge on the west side of the River Test. The records of Winchester College, which owned much property in Romsey, refer to a pub called the *Cart Wheel* being in the occupation of Thomas Lacey in 1821, and indicate that it was later the *Horse and Jockey*.

The difficulty is that evidence for the *Horse and Jockey* (under that name) goes back to the mid-1700s, though there is no specific record to contradict the 1821 statement about Thomas Lacey.

## 15 (Catherine Wheel, The Hundred **)
*(see the Sawyers Arms)*

Very little is known about the *Catherine Wheel*. Robert Carter was the licensee in 1792 and 1798.

The Catherine wheel was the trade sign of carpenters and joiners, so it is likely that there was a connection between this pub and the one that was even more obviously named as the *Sawyers Arms*. The latter can be positively located at 95 The Hundred, but there is a gap in continuity between the 1790s and 1890.

## 16 Coachmakers Arms, Latimer Street **

Facing the Lortemore Place carpark is No 33 Latimer Street, a brick-fronted house. Behind the façade, this is a timber-framed building dating back to the mid-17th century with a long history as business premises. Before becoming a private residence, it had a variety of uses and for a short while was a pub, or at least a beer house in Victorian times.

In 1867, Tom Pomeroy was in business in Latimer Street as both a coach builder and beer retailer, and it seems likely that it was at these premises – hence the name. By 1885, Tom Pomeroy had given way to George Edward Lucas, beer retailer and carriage builder, who was definitely in No 33. George Lucas had probably died by 1898 when Mrs Caroline Lucas was listed simply as beer retailer. Later, Frank Lucas, the coach builder, shoed horses under the archway, but the association with beer retailing had gone. At various times the property was also used as a baker's, a butcher's and a hardware store.

*No 33 Latimer Street, formerly The Coachmakers Arms*
*The old carriage entrance on the left now leads through to a courtyard*
*development of several houses in the old pub yard*

There must have been rebuilding in 1846 as researchers noticed a brick giving this date set high into an outside wall. Below the building is a brick cellar with some very narrow bricks and brick archways.

At the turn of the 21$^{st}$ century, the premises – which had stood empty for some time – were renovated, with new properties being built in the old yard at the rear. The whole complex was then named Coachmakers Mews.

## 17 Compton Arms **

This pub is a complete mystery. The only reference to it comes in the Directory of 1784, with John Jeffery listed as the proprietor. There is no further evidence from any source, so its existence remains problematical.

## 18 (Cricketers Arms, Crampmoor Lane **)
*(see the Old House at Home, Crampmoor)*

This may have been an earlier name for the *Old House at Home* at Crampmoor. In the 1970s, the painted wall sign for the *Old House at Home* still showed signs of an earlier underpainting that appeared to proclaim the premises as the *Cricketers Arms*.

## 19 Cross Keys, 11 Bell Street **

This is one of Romsey's old pub buildings with parts of it dating back to the

15th or 16th century. The name *'Cross Keys'* has been unchanged since the early 17th century, when Richard Ivyleafe was in occupation, perhaps as an innkeeper. He seems to have been succeeded by John Bingham whose will definitely declares him to be an 'innholder'.

John Bingham died in 1686, and his inventory suggests that he was rather a dandy. Out of an estate valued at about £80 his clothing was valued at £10. It is worth comparing this with the mere £2 worth of clothes assessed in the inventory of John Hacke, who was John Bingham's contemporary at the nearby *Bell Inn*, a more substantial hostelry.

*Side of the old Cross Keys public house looking back towards Bell Street*

An indenture made later in 1686 for the property adjacent to the *Cross Keys* on the south side indicates that Mary Bingham, widow, was carrying on her late husband's business. Presumably it still operated under the name of the *Cross Keys* but this is not stated.

Certainly, however, the name was recorded in the early 1700s. The Borough Accounts for 1735 include the following item:

'Paid the Coroner for coming to sit on a soldier that died at the
*Cross Keys*                                        10s 6d
Paid J. Mayor for going for the Coroner      2s 0d
        Jury                                           6s 8d'

Although not in the same league as the nearby *Bell Inn*, which in the turnpike era enjoyed the prestige of being a posting stage for public and private coaches, trade at the *Cross Keys* must have been reasonably prosperous. S. Moody was the innkeeper there in 1818, when he felt it worth his while to advertise his business in the *The Salisbury & Winchester Journal*. Another indication of the *Cross Keys'* level of moderate success is that the licensees did not publicise themselves as carrying on other businesses, as was the case of struggling houses, where the men's wives

48

were the licensees and the selling of beer a secondary income. The only exception seems to have been William Wilkins, who in the mid-19th century advertised his services as a castrator.

The *Cross Keys* appears to have been fairly settled in the 19th century, when some of the coaching inns that depended on long distance travellers were beginning to struggle in the face of competition from the railways. William Webb arrived at the *Cross Keys* sometime in the 1850s and was still there in 1866. After an interregnum, Frank Hargreaves was landlord in 1885 for a period of at least ten years.

The property once ran back to the present Newton Lane car park, but its stables have become separated as a private residence. These stables were still thatched at the end of the 18th century, being so described in insurance records of the 1770s.

In the 1920s there was a terrible fire that destroyed the top two storeys of the *Cross Keys*. Fire appliances from Romsey and Southampton attended the fire. Neighbours tried to extinguish the blaze before the firemen arrived, and endeavoured to protect the adjoining roof. Even so, properties to the south of the *Cross Keys* and opposite were affected. Fortunately, it was day-time and there was no loss of life.

The pub closed in 1972, but the building has retained a very fine bracket on the wall, and that is well worth looking at. Currently, the side wall towards the back of the carriage way still has the long metal sign proclaiming it to be a pub belonging to Strong & Co. Ltd of Romsey.

## 20 Crown Inn, 28 Winchester Road **

When the *Crown Inn* was put on the market in 1847, the sales particulars described the property as 'Freehold Brewery including 2 malt-houses and old-established freehold inn or public house called *The Crown'*. If it was 'old-established' in 1847, the claim that it had been a coaching inn since c1820 seems justified, though the building itself appears considerably older.

Despite this, the history of the property's use as a pub cannot be traced back any earlier, though it is tempting to believe that its location would have encouraged at least an 18th-century origin. For the *Crown* was well sited on the town side of the Winchester turnpike toll house, which stood at the junction of Winchester Road and Botley Road, and close to the Andover-Redbridge Canal wharf (near the present Plaza roundabout). In 1847, it was already claiming proximity to the newly built railway station.

The 1847 sales particulars reveal the site as a complex one with associated cottages along the street front and numerous buildings to the rear, for which there were shared rights of access. The other buildings included a blacksmith's shop, and it is likely that this may have been a long-established site for a smithy. Such activities were often found on the approach roads into towns, rather as garages are today. Researchers in the early 1970s were told that, under the tarmac in the rear yard, the stone floor tapering to a drain still survived, and that in 1970 the halter rails were still evident.

The 1847 sale seems not to have proceeded, probably because of legal complications. Some years later, the same vendors (representatives of the estate of the late John Prince) placed it on the market once again with the condition that any purchase had to be via the Chancery Court, where there was an ongoing dispute between the Prince family and James Joliffe, who now lived in the home of the late John Prince.

There followed further confusion during the long ownership of Benjamin or Benny Stevens, who was earlier the licensee of the *Bishop Blaize* and who became owner of several neighbouring and scattered properties in addition to the *Crown*. His first will, drafted in 1871, left his estate to his widow and daughter, with a proviso that the *Crown* should not be leased to a brewer or wine & spirit merchant. His final will was made in 1887, the year of his death, when he left everything in trust for the support of his two grandsons, Benjamin and Joseph Newman.

In that same year, despite the earlier proviso, the inn was leased to David Faber, brewer and wine & spirit merchant trading as Strong & Co. Ltd. The lease was converted into a freehold in 1906, but the trust complications of Benjamin Stevens' will meant that Strong's only finally purchased the property in 1920 after further recourse to the Chancery Court.

*The old Crown Inn, now offices*

Since the *Crown* was a substantial house in the parish of Romsey Extra, it was occasionally used by the Coroner for inquests. One such took place in 1911 on a week-old baby. It had been in bed with its parents at Botley Cottages, Botley Road, and had suffocated.

A set of early fairy lights survived into the 1970s. When all ablaze with lighted candles they must have looked charming. At the end of a succession of Strong's tenants, the last licensee was Nigel Keel, who was the Station Officer for Romsey Fire Brigade for a time. The inn closed in 1970.

For some time afterwards the old inn served as an antique shop called *Crown Antiques* with the old *Crown Inn* sign still hanging on the bracket. This was variously said to be the original one or one painted on copper that was beaten and flattened from brewing equipment used in the house. The property has since been converted into offices.

## 21 Dead House **
(see the Good Intent)

This was undoubtedly a nick-name applied to some beer house, though which is not clear. One rumour says that it was the beer house at 3 The Hundred, but that one may have been the *Good Intent*. Another rumour puts the *Dead House* next to the *Bridge Tavern* at Mainstone. Both stories are quite uncorroborated. However, perhaps the rumour about The Hundred is the better founded, because it is said the shop was Stares' Beer House, which was vacated when Mr Stares took over Mr Hall's beer house in Latimer Street.

## 22 Delve Inn, 42 Mill Lane *

This house was on the west corner of Church Lane and Mill Lane. It shared its name with Delve Place, the row of cottages to the south within Church Lane, and links back to an old field name.

The *Delve* had been merely a beer house in 1855, but appears to have had a full licence when it closed in 1911. By then, it belonged to Strong & Co. Ltd and was closed because it was so near the *Thatched Cottage* and the *Star*, which were also Strong's houses. It seems probable that the name *Delve Hotel* was a sarcastic local name for a modest drinking establishment.

*The one-time Delve Inn*

There were two bars, the Saloon and the Bar. The Saloon was entered from Church Lane and was intended for ladies. To obtain a drink they went up four steps and knocked on a connecting trap door. Thus they could be served discreetly. The Bar, on the other side of the house, was patronised by male drinkers.

## 23 (Dog/The Doghouse, 68 Cherville Street **)
(see the Dog & Star and the Lord Nelson)

This pub appears in the Land Tax Records between 1800 and 1804. It obviously had a turbulent few years. In 1800 it belonged to the heirs of Galpin. The tenant was J. Trandall, and the tax 4s. 7d. In 1803, the proprietor was J. Latham, and his tenant was S. Moody – the Land Tax being 4s. 9d. The *Dog* seems to have been an abbreviation for the *Dog and Star*. By 1804 it had become the *Doghouse*, and in 1806 it seems to have become the *Lord Nelson*.

51

## 24 (Dog and Star, 68 Cherville Street **)

*(see the Dog and the Lord Nelson)*

This was an early name for the *Dog*, later the *Lord Nelson*. Records relating to John Latham, the Romsey brewer who became a bankrupt in 1817, show a clear connection between the three names. They also take the history of this modest pub back at least to 1753, when the *Dog and Star* was occupied by George Warden the younger. It is possible that the use of the premises as a pub may stretch back a further decade. In 1743 the property, newly subdivided, was bought by Ambrose Waldron of Southampton, an innholder, but there is no mention in the deeds of any pub operating on the site.

Interestingly, there was a stable and weaving shop adjoining, which may suggest that a weaving family developed a sideline as drink retailers when the cloth trade diminished in the 18th century. It was in a promising location on the edge of the built-up area of that time, where it would attract people coming in from nearby villages from the north as well as those living nearby.

By 1770, the name had been shortened to the *Dog*, as given in the will of Solomon Bedford senior of Stockbridge who made the following bequest. 'Also I give and bequeath unto my daughter Jone Stevens the house at Romsey known by the sine of the *Dog* to her during her life ...'

The *Dog and Star* was, incidentally, one of the Cherville Street properties that owed a quit rent to the lord of the manor of Rockbourne (near Fordingbridge). This makes a fascinating link back to the possible medieval origins of Cherville Street as a planned development.

## 25 Dolphin, 9 The Cornmarket *

There is an impressive Regency façade to the building that was once the *Dolphin Hotel*. But older Tudor bricks in the cellar had long suggested a greater age for the basic structure, and a complete refurbishment of the property at the beginning of the 21st century also revealed previously hidden early timber work. This physical evidence fits in well with the written records that tell how the front of the existing building was greatly altered in 1828.

In its earliest form, the *Dolphin* site would have been prominent over a considerably wider area than now, for the Market Place was originally much more open. Most of the buildings in the central triangle did not exist, and many buildings around the perimeter have encroached. Local historian, Mrs Suckling of Highwood House, writing in 1915, was informed that a Mr Elcombe could remember the last man to be put in the stocks. This had occurred in 1782, and the stocks had been near the *Dolphin*, which was thus at the heart of civic events.

A detailed description of the *Dolphin* in the early 1800s is given in the Latham Bankruptcy sales particulars for his estate. This obviously relates to the property before the major alterations of a decade later.

> Lot 12    The Dolphin
> The lease of a valuable inn, called the *Dolphin*, with a messuage or tenement, and workshop adjoining, and the outhouses, yard and garden behind the same; situate in the Cornmarket, Romsey; … The *Dolphin* is now in the occupation of Mr Self, at the yearly rent of £30 who holds the same under an agreement to quit on receiving three months notice.

> The tenement and workshop adjoining are now in the occupation of Mr Clark, as a yearly tenant, at the rent of £10 pa; … The premises comprised in this Lot are held for a term of 21 years of which 10 years were unexpired at Michaelmas last, at the yearly rent of £150 payable half yearly. The lease contains a proviso for re-entry, in case of non-payment of rent for 21 days; and covenants, on the part of the lessee, for due payment of the rent; for payment of all rates and tenants taxes; for keeping the premises in repair; and covenant by the lessor for payment of the quit rent land tax and other landlords' taxes and for peaceable possession; and mutual covenants between the parties for determining the term at the end of the first fourteen years at the option of the lessee and for permitting the lessee to take down the messuage or tenement at the east end of the *Dolphin* and erect a new messuage.

This final option suggests that the property to the east of the inn was in great need of attention. Although the new owner, Thomas Figes, did not seek a full rebuild on the site, he quickly planned a substantial new façade that linked together the whole range of buildings from the town stream on the east through to the west end of the inn. He had to make several applications before finally getting permission to proceed in 1828. The work that then took place resulted in the overall appearance of the building today, though later alterations to the eastern building (subsequently in separate ownership) have destroyed the one-time unity of the elegant façade.

The *Dolphin* seems to have been the home of a number of old Romsey families at various times. Around 1800, for example, the *Dolphin* was in the hands of the Young family. They were auctioneers as well as innkeepers, and frequently held auction sales at the Dolphin. The Youngs appear to have severed their proprietorship of the *Dolphin* in 1810 because in that year an advertisement appeared in *The Salisbury and Winchester Journal* saying that the *Dolphin Inn* was to let. It was described as:

> 'The well known and long established Inn called the *Dolphin*, most advantageously situated in the Corn Market, in the town of Romsey. Now in full trade. Immediate possession may be had and further particulars known by applying (if by letter post paid) to Messrs Dorman and Warner, Solicitors, Romsey'.

Nevertheless, a later connection between the *Dolphin* and the Youngs' name occurred in 1852, when a Mr Young, carrier, called daily at 9am on his way

53

to Southampton. Mr Young was also the licensee of the *Fox Inn*. Another old Romsey family had connections with the *Dolphin* in 1852. Moody, the carrier to Lymington, called on Tuesdays and Fridays.

It is necessary, though, to be careful about names as so many first names were repeated in successive generations and even occasionally in the same. Furthermore, sometimes there was no obvious connection between different branches.  For example, another *'Dolphin'* name, Cole, occurs all over Romsey, but the Coles were not all related. There were at least two distinct branches in the town.  Confusion particularly arises regarding Mary Ann Cole, who was licensee at the *Dolphin* in the 1860s. At about the same time there was a Mary Ann Cole, widow of Henry Cole, at the *Kings Head*. This may be a coincidence of names or one lady might have held both licences.

By 1880 a third Romsey family, the Edwards, was at the *Dolphin*. John Edwards was there for at least twenty years.  An old photo of the house survives showing that it was also the Revenue Office in his day.  There was also a *Dolphin* Tap Bar, which at various times was in the lower building to the east of the carriage entrance or in outbuildings to the rear.

By the late 19th century, the *Dolphin* was a tied house of Strong & Co. Ltd., who ran an Off-Licence in the lower part of the *Dolphin*.  At one time this part was the Tory headquarters during elections for MPs.

*Dolphin Hotel, 1899*

The *Dolphin* underwent several changes of ownership after the Strong's era. It also suffered many changes of style in terms of decoration; when the first edition of this book was written in the early 1970s the paintwork was a very striking brown and orange.

As the 21st century began, the *Dolphin* experienced a complete change.  It ceased to be a public house, and was incorporated into the Bradbeers Department Store.  The inn bracket remains on the refurbished façade but now displays a Bradbeers sign, with all reference to the *Dolphin* eradicated.

*Editorial Note:  A great deal more information about the Dolphin and its inhabitants may be found in 'Bradbeers, the Story of a Department Store' by Phoebe Merrick (LTVAS 2003).*

54

## 26 (Duke of Cumberland)
*(see the Dukes Head)*

The *Duke of Cumberland* was an early name for the *Dukes Head*. Confirmation is found in 1875 sales particulars drawn up after the death of Mrs Catherine Hall of the Island, Greatbridge. The description mentions an even earlier name for this pub – the *Admiral Vernon* – a reference that has not been found anywhere else.

## 27 Dukes Head, Greatbridge
*(see the Duke of Cumberland)*

It is said that the 'Duke' was the Duke of Cumberland, as suggested by its earlier name. The licensee in the 1970s claimed that there had been an inn on the site from at least 1583 but further research is needed to endorse this. Certainly, the building is very old with a multitude of beams, and customers may enjoy an interesting chimney with a series of vents in the brickwork. The house was originally thatched. Because of the danger of flooding from the river, the cellar is shallow. Probably the water table is high too.

If the pub really has been in existence since the 16th century, then the *Dukes Head* is old even by Romsey standards. Undoubtedly, it stood on a very good site for a pub, as the historic roads to Romsey from Stockbridge and Salisbury converged by a crossing point on the Test.

*The Dukes Head, Greatbridge*

Access to the old Timsbury Bridge ran along the north side of the the the *Dukes Head* until both road and bridge were relocated in 1911. [As regards the importance of this site, it must be remembered that Old Sarum Lane, running past Roke Manor, was the main route from Romsey to Salisbury until Middlebridge was rebuilt in the 1770s and the Southampton to Salisbury turnpike connection was cut through Green Hill beyond.]

Until 1748 the house was called the *Three Tuns*, which must have led to confusion with the pub of the same name in Middlebridge Street. When alterations were made to the *Dukes Head* in the 1970s, a couple of pennies dated 1621 were found, apart from the inevitable clay pipes.

In 1784 George Bare was the licensee and in 1800 James Norris was both proprietor and mine-host. He paid £1 4s 7d land tax – a large sum by

Romsey pub standards. The rate stayed the same until 1828 when it was reduced to £1.

The Cole family – or one of them – appears out here. In 1855, *The Romsey Register* newspaper recorded the death of Mr William Cole, formerly of the *Dukes Head*. In 1879, the body of George Hall of Romsey – a suicide - was removed from the River Test and taken to the *Dukes Head* nearby.

For the benefit of the very thirsty, there existed a beer house in one of the three cottages next to the *Dukes Head*. These cottages have now been demolished.

## 28 (Falcon Inn, Church Street)
*(see the Market Inn and Abbey Hotel)*

The earliest known reference for the *Falcon Inn* appears in the Winchester College Muniments, where an indirect mention indicates that the inn existed in 1734. A century later, in 1835, another document from the same source describes a section of a property as being 'lately newly built and part of *The Falcon*'. This apparently refers to the southern section of the *Falcon*, which formed an extension hived off from property belonging to Winchester College. This explains why the College held deeds relating to the inn. The northern section was held as a freehold, and was probably the older building described by Charles Spence in his 1862 *Essay on Romsey Abbey*.

Charles Spence described the *Falcon* thus:
> 'It is probable that, among the domestic buildings of the town of Romsey, many relics of the olden time are yet to be met with. The *Falcon Inn*, in Church Street, is one of them; and it is only recently that modern convenience has sacrificed therein a fine old English hall, the chestnut groinings of which, springing from corbel-heads beautifully carved and gilt, may yet be seen in a lumber-loft. This hall has not been destroyed, but, by means of flooring and partitions, made to consist of several apartments.'

These alterations were presumably part of a long-term refurbishment of the inn, which began with the extension to the south, and which adapted the older section to the requirements of the day.

Sadly, the hall was then truly destroyed by the end of the 19th century, when the *Falcon*, under its later name of the *Market Inn*, was victim of a road-widening scheme aimed at improving the flow of traffic in and out of the Market Place.

Until this time the northern section of the *Falcon* had clearly been one of Romsey's very old buildings, though its actual use before the 18th century is uncertain. Just as uncertain is the date at which the name of the *Falcon* was changed to the *Market Inn*. The dates of individual landlords do not help; indeed they only add to the confusion since there is an incompatible overlap between the two.

There is no problem about James Bishop being landlord of the *Falcon* in 1784, James Cribb in 1823, or Thomas Reeves in 1852. But then the James Cribb name is repeated in 1855 and 1857 at a time when Henry Wheeler and Robert Floyd were appearing as landlords of the *Market Inn* (in 1855). The last mentioned *Falcon* landlord was William Quarterman who was said to be there in 1859. This is a discrepancy that needs further enlightenment. By the time that the 1867 OS Map (1:500) was produced the inn was very firmly labelled as the *Market Inn*.

## 29 Fleming Arms, Station Road *

*The old Fleming Arms building*

In the 1970s, when the first edition of this work was being prepared, the *Fleming Arms* was the youngest surviving pub in Romsey. It was only established in 1869 on land leased from the Fleming family who were the Lords of the Manor of Romsey Extra. The building bore their coat of arms, but the Fleming association has been lost since the pub closed in the late 1980s, and the building converted into offices.

As a pub, the *Fleming Arms* was a typical Victorian corner development with a curve at the junction of Alma Road and Station Road. It was an obvious site for a new pub in the mid-19th century, being close to the railway station. Its opening coincided with the early years of the second railway line through Romsey, the Andover to Southampton connection. At the time it was also convenient for the fairground and cricket ground in Alma Road.

The leasehold deed stipulated that the land in question must be enclosed by a wall or close fence six feet high. Furthermore, all outbuildings had to be screened from the view of both passers-by and neighbouring houses. Only one dwelling house was to be erected and the developers were 'not to have religious meetings or build a church or chapel or a slaughterhouse or any offensive trade'.

The builder of the *Fleming Arms*, James Feltham, was the licensee there for over ten years. His wife died in a tragic accident in 1879, when her night clothes caught fire. In his day, Mr Feltham was a dealer in building materials, a timber merchant, sawmill proprietor and victualler. Clearly being a builders' merchant was not an offensive trade – although he may have carried on that side of the business elsewhere. He cannot have had much leisure!

The building was extended southwards along Alma Road in 1894 when a billiards room was built. The stables in this area used to have the horses' names over the doors.

During World War I the building was out of bounds to troops, but in the Second World War troops were quartered in the billiards room and officers in the bedrooms. The officers all caught measles and were nursed by Mrs Richards – the wife of 'Copper' Richards, then licensee.

## 30 (Fleur de Lis/Flower de Luce **)
*(see the Bricklayers Arms)*

It seems likely that the *Fleur de Lis* and the *Flower de Luce* were one and the same. Under one name it appears in a 1784 directory with Mrs Hodges as proprietor, and under the other name it turns up in an 1823 directory with James Moore as proprietor. No address was given, and the pub did not feature by name in the Land Tax records.

Consequently, the *Fleur de Lis* was identified only as another ghost pub in 1974, and was only firmly located in 2005. Research in the schedule attached to the 1819 Tithe Allocation Map then revealed that the *Fleur de Lis* was an early name for the *Bricklayers Arms* in Banning Street. At that time it was owned by a small Romsey brewery known as Figes and Longcroft. (The Figes family was long associated with the brewery at the *Old Thatches* in Mill Lane.)

## 31 Fox Inn, Old Southampton Road **

The *Fox Inn* stood on the old Tudor road to Southampton where Palmerston Street once continued across the Romsey by-pass into the present Broadlands Park (to the left of the main gates). The *Fox* was of uncertain date but may have started as a pub in the mid-1700s after the road had become part of the turnpike road from Salisbury to Southampton. The pub may then have attracted a reasonable amount of business, being fairly close to the actual turnpike barrier.

*The old Southampton road*
*This road ran south through*
*Broadlands Park*

*The Fox Inn was roughly where*
*the estate house now stands.*

58

The inn was certainly recorded in 1784 when Thomas Webb was innkeeper. The *Fox* also featured in the sale of John Latham's property after his bankruptcy in 1817.  It was included in a single lot with the *Dolphin*, being described as '... a public house, called the *Fox*, with the outhouses and garden thereto belonging, situate near the Southampton Turnpike gate in Romsey. .... the *Fox* is now in the occupation of Mr Judd, at the yearly rent of £20 who holds the same under an agreement to quit on receiving three months notice'.

By 1819, the schedule for the tithe allocation map shows that the *Fox* was in the ownership of Romsey brewers Figes and Longcroft.  In the 1850s, John Pester Young held the licence and it is worth speculating whether he was related to the Youngs who were at the *Dolphin* before 1810.  He lived at the *Fox Inn* with his wife, her mother, their five-year-old daughter, a niece, a son and a lodger.  Soon afterwards Francis Jesser took over the business. He may have been one of the Jesser and Cressey brewing family although he supplemented his income by working as a wheelwright.

In the 1860s, however, Lord Palmerston negotiated with the Andover to Southampton railway company for the road to be diverted further away from his home to its present more easterly route.  Within Broadlands Park, the old road became a private way south of the By-pass roundabout, its entrance still clearly visible to the left of the main gates to the Park.  Only a small section of the old Southampton road survived to the north of Broadlands Park.  It was first renamed Park Street, and subsequently Palmerston Street, as it remains today.

Lord Palmerston then bought and pulled down the *Fox Inn*.  Probably the trade was in decline by then, since the railway steadily reduced the number of road travellers during the 19<sup>th</sup> century.

The *Fox Inn* was undoubtedly older than the nearby Fox Mill on the north-eastern corner of the Broadlands roundabout.  This mill was only created in the late 1790s after waste water from the new Andover-Southampton canal ensured sufficient head of water to drive a waterwheel.  The mill presumably took its name from the pub.  In the 1970s, some claimed that they could remember seeing the foundations of the *Fox Inn* not long before.

# 32 (Globe, Mill Lane **)
*(see the Volunteer)*

This name seems to have belonged to a very modest beer house as there are no advertisements for it.  It has been described as being in the house by the bridge, and clearly needs further investigation.  It may have been an alternative name for the *Volunteer*, which stood on the north side of Mill Lane, a little before the modern Holman Drive.

For a while at least, possibly in the 1850s, the *Globe* was run by a Mr Floyd. His wife ruined any reputation the house may have had hitherto by making her rooms available to women with dubious morals. A succession of male visitors created a very undesirable reputation for the Floyds and their beer-shop. When Elizabeth Goddard, one of their helpers, later made an affidavit against them, she related some of the unsavoury events she had witnessed.

After a while the Floyds, with Elizabeth helping them to move, transferred their licence to the *Angel* in Bell Street, where they continued 'business as before'.

## 33 Good Intent, The Hundred **

It has been alleged that this was the name given to No 3 The Hundred when it was a beer house. Mr Kersey, proprietor of the long-established jewellery business at that address, said in the 1970s that there certainly had been a beer house there, and that a clause in his deed stipulated that no alcoholic beverages should be sold on the premises. This was probably because the vendor was moving to a new pub and did not want competition with his old house. Restrictive clauses of various sorts were not uncommon in Romsey.

*The possible site of the Good Intent*

On the question of the name, many beer houses gave themselves a name which was sometimes used and sometimes not. Alternatively, the locals often gave a place a nickname. Either of these explanations is possible.

## 34 Ham and Sickle **
(see the Mallet and Chisel)

## 35    Hatchet **

There is only one known reference to this pub, and that relates to 1686. At that time the victualler was a certain William Ives, who was murdered by his wife and her lover, John Noyse. A fuller account is given on page 12 of the introduction. The pub may have been on a corner of Newton Lane, probably the north side.

## 36    Horse and Jockey, 23 Mainstone **
(formerly called Middlebridge Street)
*(see the Cart Wheel, Middlebridge Street/Mainstone)*

The *Horse and Jockey* seems to have been one of the many Romsey pubs that evolved as a result of the growth of the coaching trade in the mid-18th century – although the building could be far older. It has been suggested that the house was once known as the *White Hart* but this is rather unlikely because both names existed at the same time.

*An early drawing of the Horse and Jockey
showing now vanished houses and the turning to Whiteparish beyond*

The building has two of the projecting bay windows so typical of older Romsey pubs. There used to be many more such windows than there are now, but, in the 19th century, the Pavement Commissioners were instrumental in having a number of them removed as obstructions. Many years later, in 1974, a car was successful where the Pavement Commissioners had failed, and demolished one of the windows in a spectacular accident. Fortunately, it was then rebuilt. Even more fortunately, the house was then no longer licensed, for the window in question had been a favourite seat amongst the regulars.

The earliest reference to the *Horse and Jockey* came in 1797 when Michael Molloy told the Mayor how his grandfather married a person called Mary Bedford who at that time kept the sign of the *Horse and Jockey* in the parish of Romsey Extra and that 'he had heard his mother say that his father was born in the said parish of Romsey Extra'. Molloy's age is not recorded although he was an adult so at the very least his grandmother would have been at the *Horse and Jockey* in the mid-1700s. Perhaps Mary Bedford's business began as a comparatively small one, which then benefited from its prime site at the foot of Pauncefoot Hill on the approach to Middlebridge and the town centre.

A number of familiar names are to be found in the annals of the *Horse and Jockey*. Richard Cole lived there in 1838 though not necessarily as licensee. In 1878, Tom Webb was to be found there. By 1880, the licensee was John Matthews, a smith and wheelwright. The pub closed in 1972, and the house was converted into a veterinary surgery in 1973.

A couple of decades later and the veterinary surgery moved across the road, and the *Horse and Jockey* re-opened as a pub. The old and very large pub  sign was fixed once again high on the side wall where it could be seen at some distance by travellers coming down Pauncefoot Hill. A new lease of life seemed assured, but unfortunately it was short-lived. As the 21$^{st}$ century opened the building had been thoroughly refurbished and re-invented as the Brasseria *Casa Bodega*, a licensed restaurant.

*Brasseria Casa Bodega, formerly the Horse & Jockey*

## 37 Hunters Inn, Woodley
*(see the [Old] Rising Sun)*

The *Hunters* Inn has been a tied house for a very long time. Indeed, there is no evidence that brewing was ever carried out on the premises, and the house belonged to Mr Trodd of Trodd and Hall Brewery at the beginning of the 19$^{th}$ century. The land was part of the Fleming Estate as late as 1819.

*The Hunters Inn*

62

Mr Trodd changed the name of the place from the *Old Rising Sun*, which must have saved a good deal of confusion with the *Sun* at the bottom of Winchester Hill. However, there seems to have been a partial return to the old name in the mid-19th century. Although the house was the *Hunters Inn* in the 1830s, it had become the *Rising Sun* in the 1850s, and then was the *Hunters Inn* again by the end of the century.

In fact, it seems to have settled back into its present name by 1875, when it was sold as a tied pub of The Horsefair Brewery. The rental valuation of these freehold premises was then £21, a high sum compared with some of the other pubs on offer at the time. The *Hunters* was some way outside Romsey at that time, and several decades would pass before the town boundary moved out close to it.

When the Hunters Inn was sold towards the end of the 19th century, it was described as:

~~~~~~~

A FREEHOLD PUBLIC-HOUSE
Known as 'THE HUNTER'S INN''
(Formerly 'The Rising Sun')
Situate at Woodley, about one-and-a-half miles from Romsey, on the Winchester Road, and in the Parish of Romsey-extra, containing Bar, Parlour, Public-room, Tap-room, Kitchen, and Cellar, five rooms over,
Stabling for four horses, Skittle-alley,
KITCHEN GARDEN AND TWO PADDOCKS,
In all about 1a. 2r. 0p. (more or less). In the occupation of G. Parker

~~~~~~~

Although the building's use as a pub cannot be traced back further than the 1790s, the main part is certainly more than 200 years old. There is a very large brick fireplace in the parlour with what is described as a 'little tunnel' at the side; there were once two bars with a brick wall between them, but this was removed. It must have been very inconvenient for the landlord to move from one bar to the other for serving – it being necessary to negotiate steps and cross the shallow cellar. The entrance to the house had a brick floor, the tap room a stone floor and the parlour a wood floor. The older part of the house used to be thatched and there was once a large shed with stables and a coach house.

During the First World War one licensee lost his licence for selling beer to children.

As the 21st century began, the *Hunters Inn* had become a family orientated pub. One of the two paddocks had become a children's play area, while the other had been converted into the essential modern requirement of a car park. The kitchen garden was still in existence with considerable emphasis on pumpkin growing. (The pub featured an annual pumpkin festival.) The skittle alley was no more, perhaps converted into the kitchen or the more convenient ground floor 'cellar'.

63

Inside, the fireplace with the 'little tunnel' remained but the semi-circular bar gave access to all the interlinked bar areas. To the rear and slightly raised up steps was a roomy dining area looking out over the garden.

## 38 Kings Head, 80 The Hundred *

Part of this old establishment is Tudor. It is thought that the house was used as a Workhouse for historic Romsey Extra at the end of the Tudor period. The women's ward was in this building that later became the *Kings Head*, and the men's ward was in an adjacent building. Allegedly there was a bridge between the two upon which a guard was placed.

*Berties Restaurant*
*formerly the Kings Head*

As with so many of Romsey's hostelries, records of this building's role as a pub date from the 18th century, when the town was growing in response to the trade brought by the new turnpike roads. In this case, the site was very advantageous, being at the junction of The Hundred (leading to the east) with what was then the way to Southampton (now Palmerston Street) turning off to the south. In a Bill of Sale of 1842 the house was described as being commodious and well frequented, with a good situation for trade.

For many years there was a hidden room in the *Kings Head*, and this was reached through a door in a fireplace and up a flight of stairs. The room was soundproofed with cork and leaf mould to a depth of ten inches. Around the walls were banners with crests on them. Who used this room or when or why is not known. All traces of the sound-proofing and the banners were destroyed when the pub was modernised in the 20th century. The banners were apparently so old that they were crumbling away.

64

In 1927, Georgian coins and pieces of Roman and pre-Roman pottery were found beside or underneath the building. On other occasions a boar's tusk and some pieces of rock were found. The deeds stipulated that twenty soldiers had to be billeted in an upstairs room 'on demand', a clause often found regarding licensed premises.

The property was in the hands of the Withers family in the 17th and 18th centuries, and in 1792 was tenanted by Mrs Wools. She may have been the widow of William Wools who was there in 1784.

Members of the Wools family may be traced intermittently throughout the 17th, 18th and early-19th centuries, and where locations are given in the records they seem to be centred in The Hundred. As well as innkeepers (at the *Phoenix* as well as the *Kings Head*), they were blacksmiths or working in allied metal-working trades. Names and dates often coincide, and it may be that smithing was taking place as ancillary activities behind the pub buildings, which were certainly well-located for this type of business.

For many years in the 19th century the Cole family were at the *Kings Head*. First of all, there was James Cole from 1842, then Henry Cole and subsequently Mary Ann Cole who was Henry's widow. In Mary Ann Cole's day, the inn was also a posting house. Trade must have been good because the Census of 1851 shows Henry Cole, his wife, adult daughter and a male and female servant living there.

## 39 Lamb Chop **
(see the Mallet and Chisel)

## 40 Lamb Inn, 7 Mainstone **
## [or Middlebridge Street]

The *Lamb* was conveyed to two Romsey brewers, Samuel Elliot and Charles Isdell, in 1779, though whether it traded under the name of the *Lamb* at that date is uncertain. The first known licensee was George Holloway in 1784; it is worth speculating whether his descendants ran the *Woolpack*.

In 1795, Elliott and Isdell sold out their entire business to a newly acquired partner, John Latham, and in the agreements drafted at the time the pub was described as:

> 'All that messuage or Tenement bearing the sign of the *Lamb* situate standing and being in a certain street called [blank] Street near to a certain Bridge called Middlebridge in the Parish of Romsey Extra aforesaid together with the garden stable brewhouse backside outhouses skittle alley and appurtenances thereunto belonging late in the tenure or occupation of John Pitter but now of William Winn victualler.'

Despite being sandwiched in the short stretch between the *Horse and Jockey* and the *Bridge Tavern*, this inn managed to survive for a long time, though

65

it was very unobtrusive for several decades.  It probably relied mainly on local regulars and passing carters and travellers from nearby villages.  Its side entrance and stabling gave the *Lamb* an advantage over the *Bridge Tavern*.

Another old Romsey family name occurred here in the late 1850s, when Samuel Moody was the licensee.  It was during his time that the *Lamb Inn* was mentioned in a Court case arising from trouble on Fair Day of 27th August.  Other evidence suggests that, at that time, the Fair was held in the meadows behind Mainstone or the Causeway.

The *Lamb* was one of those owned by The Horsefair Brewery when that concern was sold in 1875.  The sales particulars describe it as follows:

~~~~~~~

## A FREEHOLD BEER-HOUSE
### Known as 'THE LAMB'

Situate near Middle Bridge, in the town of Romsey, and containing Bar, Tap-room, Parlour, Scullery, Cellar, and three rooms above; Yard, Stabling for four horses and loft over. In the occupation of Mr J. Carpenter.

~~~~~~~

Rather surprisingly for an unpretentious beer-house, its annual rental value was given as £9 10s 0d, but this probably reflects the unusually large plot behind.

The last discovered reference to this pub as a going concern gives the name of Alfred Baker as the licensee in 1883, when the property was described in sales particulars as follows:

> *Lot 2 is*
> The Freehold Beerhouse and Premises known as *"The Lamb"* situate near Middlebridge, Romsey [adjoining property belonging to Lord Mount Temple]
> Now in the occupation of Mr Alfred Baker, under a quarterly agreement, at the very low rent of £10 per annum, tenant paying rates and taxes.  The House contains Bar, Tap room, Sitting Room, Scullery, Cellar, &c, on the ground floor, and 4 rooms above.  In the yard behind is stabling for 4 horses, loft, brick and slated cart house, wood and coal stores, WC, &c, and a piece of garden ground.
> The licence of this lot might be made available for transfer, and the property would readily let at a higher rent without it, the present rental being nominal in consequence of its being a brewer's house.

No purchasers were recorded for the sale of this particular property, and the implication must surely be that its closure would not be a matter for regret.  Eventually, indeed, the *Lamb* became a common lodging house after losing its licence.  A night's lodging cost 4d.  That was in the time of Mrs Young who was the widow of the previous tenant.

The house has since been rebuilt (see page 2), but an image of the old pub lives on in a large painting of Mainstone that is displayed in Romsey Town Hall, and in an old photograph (see page 2). The old pictures show the *Lamb* with a bow window on the first floor, supported by posts.

## 41 Lansdowne Arms, Church Street **

This was a late pub that had a short life-span. The house was built as a brewery in 1829. Before that there had been a grand house, perhaps medieval, on the site, which Dr John Latham (father of John Latham, the brewer) described in his work on Romsey. In the 17th century this half-timbered property had been the birthplace of Sir William Petty, a renowned polymath whose father, Anthony Petty was a Romsey cloth dyer. Sir William was the ancestor of the Marquesses of Lansdowne, one of whom installed a memorial to him in Romsey Abbey during the 1850s. It is from this family that Lansdowne Gardens in Greatbridge Road takes its name. Sir William Petty's house was destroyed by fire in 1826, but its replacement bears an elegant plaque placed there in 1987 to mark the tercentenary of his death.

*Lansdowne Arms building as shops, 1974*
*still showing pub name painted on upper part of wall*

Even before the fire, the property had an association with brewing. The Petty house fire spread to a neighbouring malt-house, which was restored by William George Lawes. These new premises were bought by Jesser and Cressey's Brewery in 1855. Brewing was subsequently discontinued on the site, and the property used solely as a pub.

The *Lansdowne Arms'* licence was withdrawn in 1911 as the house was too near both the *Star* and the *Abbey Hotel*. The tenant was an elderly widow of an old tenant and servant of the brewery. She paid no rent but would have to move if the licence were withdrawn. The Police objected to the back

67

entrance of the building although they conceded that there had been no transfer of licence nor any conviction for five years. Mrs Cecily Simmons, the tenant, received £42 10s 0d compensation; Strong's, the lessees, received £80 and the Marquess of Lansdowne, the owner, received £302 10s 0d.

The old Lansdowne Arms buildings as private houses, 2005

Subsequently, the building had several uses, being at various times a cobbler's and a baker's. In the 1970s, nevertheless, the name 'Lansdowne Arms' could still be clearly read on the front of the building. Hampshire County Council acquired the run of properties from Church Place northwards, and built the Magistrates Court (now Social Services Offices) in the 1960s on the southern part of the site. The Council then scheduled the next stretch, including the Lansdowne Arms building, for demolition to make way for a new police station. These plans never materialised and the buildings were instead converted into private residences.

## 42 Latimer Arms, 11 Latimer Street **

The Latimer Arms was one of several in a short stretch of Latimer Street. Competition may explain why the property seems often to have been the centre of a range of activities rather than simply fulfilling a role as a pub.

The building itself is very old, being timber-framed with lathe and plaster infill. On entering, it is necessary to step down into the room that opens directly onto the street, an indication of the rise of the road surface and the introduction of pavements long after the house was first built. The ground flooring is board, below which is a layer of silver sand on the earth. A copy of a Reading newspaper dated 1830 was found under the floor board.

However, the origins of the building's history as a pub seem to be only late Victorian. A report in 1916 gives a flavour of the type of pub the Latimer Arms may have been in the early 20th century. The licensee then was called Frederick Latimer, and he was fined 5s 0d for serving drinks after hours at a Christmas Party. His customers were fined 1/- each.

In 1974 it was established that the cellar, which had a stone arch, showed evidence of brewing. The lounge used to have a large open fireplace but that was removed. At the back of the garden researchers saw a wall held together with sand, without mortar or cement. In the well, one licensee found a set of pewter measuring mugs.

It is said that 'Latimer' derives from an old word meaning a slow-moving stream, and that a stream used to run down the middle of the road. This has now been filled in but accounts for the name of the pub and the street.

Surviving property documents quote a deed of 1687, which has not itself survived. It is recited as saying

'Thomas Penton did sell unto John Blatch his messuage with the backside or garden there unto … situated in the Hundred of Romsey in a street called Latimer Street on the east side of the said street between a messuage then in the possession of John Puckeridge on the north by a messuage of George Baverstock then in the possession of Stephen Ray on the south the said street on the west a garden then of widow Weeks on the east. To hold the same unto the said John Blatch … for one thousand years'.

The back reference to 1687 may have related to the setting up of a 1000-year lease, a common way of transferring property out of the public eye during the 17th century. The lessee paid a large entry fine with subsequent annual payments of a 'peppercorn' nature. This idea for the *Latimer Arms* site is supported by other references elsewhere in the deeds to a 1000-year lease being signed in 1824, when there was also mention of a gateway to the property. (Such 'perpetual' leases were sales in all but name, and at the beginning of the 20th century a law was passed enabling all these leases to be converted into freeholds.)

In 1848, the property passed to James George Bunday who subsequently erected stables and a slaughterhouse. In 1866, Edward Stares became the lessee, when he bought the property from James George Bunday and Thomas Ayres Spratt in that year.

Mr Stares proceeded to enlarge the holding. In 1876, he bought 'that messuage in the occupation of Edward Gritt' from Mr Charles Luddington Hall. Mr Gritt paid 3s 0d a week and had lived there for thirty-three years. The Halls had been left the property by an uncle, Charles John Hall of Stanbridge Earls. This suggests a link with the beer trade, for Charles John Hall was a brewer, who had married the daughter of the previous owner of Stanbridge Earls. In 1880, Mr Stares bought property to the east of his holding from Mr W.E. Godfrey, a linen draper.

In 1883, Mr Stares died. In 1902, Mr F.G.W. Mortimer, solicitor, and William Maynard, a veterinary surgeon, sold the *Latimer Arms* to W.W. Holliday, a cattle dealer. In 1915, Hester Holliday leased to Strong's Brewery 'All that messuage, dwellinghouse, beershop, dairy and store now in the occupation of the lessees … with the yard and garden at the rear, cowpens, coal sheds, stable with loft over and piggeries and appurtenances thereto'.

In 1920, Strong's bought the holding outright. In 1972, the pub closed and, after being empty for two years, the house was put on the market in 1974. Subsequently, the building was for many years the *Latimer Coffee Shop*, a popular venue in the town. Later, it turned into a wine bar and restaurant under various names, eventually entering the 21ˢᵗ century as *Judge's* restaurant and since changed to *The Olive Tree*.

*Judge's (ex-Latimer Arms) now The Olive Treee*

## 43 Leg of Mutton **
*(see the Mallet and Chisel)*

## 44 Lord Nelson, 68 Cherville Street **
*(see the Dog & Star and the Dog)*

The *Lord Nelson* started life as *the Dog & Star*, later abbreviated to the *Dog* or *Doghouse*. When John Latham, brewer, acquired this pub in 1803, it was described as 'then or lately called or known by the name of the *Dog* but then called or known by the name or sign of the *Lord Nelson* ... and then in the possession of Samuel Moody'. This seems an early date – before the Battle of Trafalgar - for a pub to be named after the great naval hero, but the document is clear on the point.

John Latham owned the *Nelson* until 1817, when it passed into the hands of the assignees of his bankruptcy. During his ownership the house had a succession of tenants, and this continued after it was acquired by other Romsey brewers - Henry Ploughman in 1819 and then Hall and Co. in 1821. At one stage in the early 19ᵗʰ century the house was called the *Nelson Ale-house* and was occupied by Elizabeth Warden.

A very clear description of the *Lord Nelson* appears in the sales particulars for the auction that followed Latham's bankruptcy.

> Lot 8    Lord Nelson
> A freehold public house, known by the sign of the *Lord Nelson*; containing three bedrooms, parlour, a good tap room, wash house, and cellar, with a new stable for five horses, and soldiers rooms over, and other outhouses, and a large garden behind the same,

with a private way through it from Priestlands; now in the occupation of Mr Hitchcock, at the yearly rent of £8 who holds the same under an agreement to quit, on receiving three months notice.
This Lot is subject to a land tax of 3s. 7d. pa and a quit rent of 5s. 0d. pa.

Half a century later, in 1875, a more meagre description appeared in the sales particulars of The Horsefair Brewery assets, when the pub was worth £10 8s 0d a year in rent.

~~~~~~~~

### A FREEHOLD BEER-HOUSE
### Known as 'THE LORD NELSON'
### (Formerly 'THE DOG')

Cherville Street, Romsey, containing four rooms on the ground floor and three rooms over, Stabling for two horses, brick shed (formerly used as a forge), good Garden. In the occupation of W. Landall.

~~~~~~~~

Apart from the hint of a blacksmith on the site, this brief description offers little new.

A further description relates:
'There is a cellar, which is approached by steep steps from the rear bar. It has flagstones and bricks on the floor. The walls are partly timbered and otherwise brick, with both a brick archway and elsewhere an alcove. One owner used to salt pork and store it in the cellar. Whenever the cellar flooded, which was frequently, the pork would float around.'

Nelson Cottage

The house was considerably altered when it became a private residence. The front parlour had large windows and a glass door. The rear parlour was entered either down two steps from the front parlour or by a side door. This door was subsequently bricked up and replaced with a small window.

# 45 Luzborough House, Luzborough Lane

*Luzborough House* is a rarity, a new pub that opened after the first edition of this book in 1974, though it is housed in a very old building. *Luzborough House* was once a farmhouse within the Broadlands estate, and subsequently became a private residence popular among the more successful businessmen of the area.

71

The last private inhabitant was Lord Mountbatten's land agent. He was Commander William Frederick George North, who died there on 8th October 1977. Luzborough House was converted into a pub in 1986.

*Luzborough House pub*

## 46    Mallet and Chisel, Squab Wood **
*(see also the Ham and Sickle, the Lamb Chop and the Leg of Mutton)*

This establishment is very controversial.  There are sufficient rumours to make it seem likely that licensed premises did exist in Squab Wood and probably also in nearby Salisbury Lane.  If it can be established that a drove road once came through Squab Wood, this explains the basis for the existence of either one or two pubs there.   Mr Shore Nightingale, who purchased Embley Park in 1826, is reputed to have closed the *Mallet and Chisel* in Squab Wood and another pub in Sherfield Road, but whether these are the same pub is not known.

The Biddlecombe family lived in Squab Wood for three hundred years and a photo exists of the last Miss Biddlecombe as a girl in her grandmother's kitchen.  This was in an old mud and wattle cottage with a thatched roof and was called the *Lamb Chop* (or *Mutton Chop*).  It lay one hundred yards to the east of the Merry Garden where Miss Biddlecombe had her tea gardens for many years.

It is suggested that for the last few years of its existence, Clem Biddlecombe sold Lovibonds' beer at the *Lamb Chop*.  At one time the annual works outing from Berthon's Boat Works was to Squab, but Strong's supplied the beer for the occasion.  Whether or not there is any connection between the *Mallet and Chisel* and the *Lamb Chop* is totally unknown.

The above seems to be the most coherent explanation of the pub or pubs in Squab Wood but there is a great mass of uncorroborated evidence – one informant says the *Mallet and Chisel* was still in business in 1854. another suggests the *Lamb Chop* was called the *Leg of Mutton*.  A third source explains that Squab Cottage was licensed as the *Woodman's Arms* and the *Ham and Sickle* was the Monk's Cottages.  A coherent history of the pubs in Squab Wood would make a subject of a separate pamphlet if the facts ever became clear enough.

## 47 (Market Inn, 11 Church Street)
*(see the Falcon and the Abbey Hotel)*

An interesting description of the *Market Inn* appears in the 1875 sales particulars for The Horsefair Brewery assets.

~~~~~~~

FREEHOLD & PART-LEASEHOLD COMMERCIAL INN
Known as 'THE MARKET INN' (formerly 'THE FALCON')
Immediately facing the Abbey, Church Street, Romsey, containing *on the Ground floor* - Bar, Parlour, Commercial-room, Tap-room, Kitchen, Scullery, Beer and Wine Cellars, Store-room, Larder, &c. *On the Upper floors* – a large room, six Bedrooms. *Outside* – Paved Yard with side entrance from street, Stabling for eight horses, Cart-shed, Skittle Alley, Quoit Ground and Garden. In the occupation of Mr Scorly [sic]/

The Leasehold portion is that part of the house which has been re-built, and is described in the lease as 'the south part of the Messuage called "The Falcon", and a narrow passage leading to the necessary house' [toilet], and is held on lease from Winchester College for a term of 30 years from Michaelmas, 1864, at a nominal rent of 5s. per annum.
The remaining portion of the Premises and Garden is FREEHOLD.

~~~~~~~

The leasehold part, being newly rebuilt, yielded an annual rent of £10 against £4 from the freehold. The *Market Inn* seems to have had its special attractions in the form of a skittle alley and a quoit ground.

*The Market Inn (extreme left) c1880s*

Four years later, *The Romsey Register* of 12th June 1879 reported that
'Mr Strong in a letter read at the Council meeting, objected to cutting through an ancient building, but is willing to facilitate the projected improvement in a liberal spirit. He will sell the Inn and

consent to its being rebuilt on a new line and offers a donation of £200 if that plan should be determined on'.
Unfortunately, Mr Strong's objection was not enough to prevent the final destruction of the historic building described by Charles Spence during the pub's days as the *Falcon*.

The need to rebuild was paramount. The inn fell within the section of Church Street scheduled for the road-widening scheme between the Market Place and Church Place. The work was being instigated by Romsey's Sanitary Authority, which had taken over the work of the old Pavement Commissions after the enlargement of Romsey Borough in 1876. The Authority managed to achieve most of its aim by 1880, a date-stone on the new Ashley Terrace bearing witness to their success in pushing back the frontage on the east side. There was then a delay due to a strange dual ownership of the *Market Inn*. Mr Strong's reluctance to endorse the demolition of an historic building related only to the northern section of the inn, which he owned; he leased the southern part, which had been a later extension, from Winchester College.

A report of a Council meeting on the subject of Church Street, in April 1879, stated that 'the present aspect of Church Street with its projecting *Market Inn*, is one which offends every eye; and no improvement can be approved of until the obstruction has been done away. Expense must of course attend its removal'. There was a delay of some years, however, before the purchase of the lease from Winchester College was satisfactorily concluded at a cost to the Corporation of £256.

Meanwhile, in May 1880, the Foresters held their annual fete, setting out from the *Market Inn* with a Brass Band and returning for a 'substantial dinner … provided by the worthy host Mr Scorey'. They then adjourned to a meadow in The Hundred for a fete. The following year seventy sat down to dinner, so the *Market Inn* must have been quite a substantial establishment. In 1898, John Scorey was still in business. He was advertising himself as a Carriage Proprietor and as having the only fully licensed free house in Romsey.

The rebuilding took place during the continued tenancy of John Scorey, and the new hostelry was renamed the *Abbey Hotel*. The earlier building line is now partially indicated by the building to the north (No 13 Church Street).

## 48 (New Inn)
*(See the Vine)*

This pub is mentioned in Pigot's Directory of 1823, but its location would be unknown if were not for the 1875 sales particulars of The Horsefair Brewery. One of the tied pubs then being sold was the *Vine* in Cherville Street. The *Vine* is very positively listed as 'Formerly *The New Inn*'.

## 49 Newton Arms, Newton Lane **

Around 1970, a photograph of an unnamed pub appeared in *The Romsey Advertiser*. The caption suggested that the building might have been the *Newton Arms*. As it happened, the guess was wrong. Older Romsonians quickly pointed out that the *Newton Arms* had had long window sills, wide enough for men to sit on them while they drank their beer. The photograph showed not the pub but an adjacent building.

Very little is known of the early history of this pub, but in 1863 it was one of the lots for sale being offered by the devisees of the late Josiah George, esquire, brewer. Mr Jenvey drew a site plan of the lots. This showed that the *Newton Arms* pub was on the south side of Newton Lane, its frontage starting some 260 feet along from the front corner of No 1 Middlebridge Street (currently occupied by Twist, the ladies' dress shop).

The plan includes a sketch of the pub's ground floor. At the street front, it shows a parlour (east) and tap room (west) either side of a central entry passage. The passage led to a door into the rear and slightly narrower block, which appears to have been the private domestic quarters. The door into this area opened directly onto the north side of a huge double fireplace. One hearth faced east into a sitting room at the south end of which there was access to a cellar. The other hearth faced west into the kitchen, which had a door to a wash house on the south side. The arrangement of this rear block, particularly the position of the central double hearth, suggests that it may have been a much earlier building than the 'pub' section at the front, perhaps a timber-framed property in the style known as a 'baffled entry'.

The pub was closed in 1917, when Mrs Martha Elizabeth Cole was the licensee. Her husband worked as a driver (of horses) for Strong's Brewery. When the pub closed she was paid £60 compensation; Strong's, the lessees, only £15; and the Executors of the late William Bentley George, the owners, £510. The link with the George family is interesting. They had been important brewers based at the southern end of Bell Street immediately to the north of the Town Mill, and with additional premises in Newton Lane. Towards the end of the 19th century, their business was absorbed into David Faber's brewing empire, Strong & Co Ltd of Romsey.

A report about the closure of the *Newton Arms* appeared in *The Romsey Advertiser*, and is probably worth quoting in full:
'Mr Jenvey, Estate Agent, produced a map showing the sites of the pubs in Romsey. He said the *Newton Arms* was in a bye street. The nearest pub, the *Angel* in Bell Street, was about 160 yards. The *Cross Keys* was about 187 yards; the *Bugle* in the Cornmarket was 225 yards. To the *Bricklayers Arms* it was about 250 yards; to the *Three Tuns* in Middlebridge Street was about 450 yards.

A ground plan of the premises was produced. The accommodation used for the licensed trade was a small barn, an irregular shaped tap room and a small cellar. The average height of the rooms was seven feet. The rest of the front of the premises was used as a shop. On the ground floor was also living accommodation. On the first floor were four bedrooms, but access to the third and fourth was by going through the other two bedrooms. There were also some other small rooms, some without windows. The second floor was four bedrooms let to a sub-tenant.

At the west end was a partly covered passage way leading to a garden. The tenants of adjoining cottages had a right of way through this passage way. Off the passage way was a urinal of 5ft 2in by 2ft 9in with no doors or screen. There were seven cottages to the south, and five cottages in Newton Lane and two cottages in the gardens adjoining the *Newton Arms* garden.

The Superintendent said there was one licence to 151½ of the population. The owners were the executors of W.G. George and it was leased to Strong and Co. The present tenant had only been in since 1914. The Rateable Value was £16.

There was nothing against the conduct of the establishment. The arrangements were bad with regard to the shop. The back access made police supervision difficult. It was referred to the Compensation Authorities.'

The site of the *Newton Arms* was more or less facing the southern end of the long building to the west of Newton Lane car park (currently a carpet shop)

Approximate site of the Newton Arms

## 50 New Wheel **

The only mention of this establishment comes in Pigot's Directory of 1823, when J. Waterman is listed as the licensee. Whether the house is the same as the Wheel, one of the Cartwheels or the Catherine Wheel is difficult to determine.

## 51 Old House at Home, Crampmoor Lane **

The property that was once Crampmoor's *Old House at Home* has now been demolished. In 1974, however, the name was still painted on the side of the house, although it had not been a pub for many years. Below the name '*Old House at Home*' appeared to be painted the words *Cricketer's Arms*, presumably an earlier name for the same establishment. This was only ever a beer house and sold home-brewed beer. In 1859, Emos Laurence held the licence. Customers were mainly the inhabitants of Crampmoor village and workers on the nearby railway. It is possible that the house not only served railway maintenance men but also those who built the railway.

*The Old House At Home, Crampmoor*

The house was a brick-built cottage with a Guardian fire insurance mark over the door, which faced away from the road. The mark depicted an angel but was undated. One or two beams showed inside so the outer walls may have been rebuilt. Running at an angle to the house was a shed. The walls of this were once constructed of thick mud but had since been largely replaced. This outhouse had been the brewery; it had previously had a thatched roof, but when the thatch was destroyed by fire it was replaced by corrugated iron.

The *Old House at Home* was a favourite spot for a lunch of bread and cheese and beer. The garden offered relaxation in the form of iron quoits for aiming at a post bedded into clay. The last licensee, Mr Vic Street, had given up the business by 1936 when he was ninety years old.

## 52   Old House at Home, Love Lane
(*see the Spotted Cow*)

The only licensee's name to occur here between 1855 and 1926 was Smith. The earliest Smith was a beer retailer and brickmaker. Later Smiths called themselves brewers and farmers and dairymen.

The last Smith – Balacker – was something of a legend in Romsey. He owned an orchard at the rear of the property and was frequently chasing out the children who entered it. He used to collect rents for the adjoining properties and it is said that people who fell into arrears were expected to drink every night in the pub. One of his tenant publicans said that glass drinking-vessels finally undermined the brewing side of the business. The trouble arose because customers had come to expect a clear brew, which Mr Smith did not supply. His recipe for beer survived until just before the first

77

edition of this work, and was remembered for the absence of finings to clear the brew. The resulting cloudiness had not been noticeable in pewter tankards.

The thatched roof is even more impressive from the rear than from the front. The core house is timber-framed and has a massive central chimney stack which used to have a bread oven. An old account book survived and included massive purchases of flour as well as the normal ingredients needed for brewing, so it may be that the Smiths included baking as a sideline.

*The Old House At Home, Love Lane*

The deeds of the house date back to 1774, and the licence is thought to be of similar age, though nothing is known of earlier licensees. In 1875, a brick-built and tiled house came on the market. This may be the younger easterly section. For many years well water used for brewing was hand-pumped to a tank above the brewhouse. The four adjoining cottages had their water from the same source. But by 1904 the well had become polluted, making both the water and the beer made from it undrinkable. Mr Smith claimed that the pollution was caused by a leaking water bay of the gas-holder at the nearby Gas Works. Although the Gas Company counter-claimed that the pollution came from Mr Smith's own drains, it had to pay for mains water to be supplied.

When Mr Smith gave up the business in 1926, the *Old House at Home* passed to Hammertons, a small brewery that was subsequently absorbed by Charringtons.

## 53    (Packhorse, The Hundred **)
*(see the Barley Mow and the Cartwheel)*

The *Packhorse* name first appears in a directory of 1839, when Robert Cole was the proprietor. It was a short-lived name for premises that once stood on the site of Alma Terrace. The pub was first recorded as the *Cartwheel* in

1795, but had changed its name to the *Barley Mow* by 1823. After an uncertain number of years as the *Packhorse*, the pub seems to have reverted to being the *Barley Mow* by the time it was pulled down in the 1860s.

## 54 (Phoenix, 32 The Hundred)
*(see The Tavern)*

The present pub building is thought to stand on the site of a much older one. The name '*Phoenix*' suggests that the building arose from the ashes of its predecessor. Mrs Suckling of Highwood House, an enthusiastic local historian writing at the end of the 19th and beginning of the 20th century, wondered whether the idea of the name Phoenix came from an old Abbey bell, now recast, that read:

> *From ashes now am turned*
> *Like Phoenix new and old am burned*

Another source has suggested that the heraldic bird that is connected with the Broadlands Estate could have been the inspiration for the name, although that bird is certainly not a phoenix.

*The Phoenix, 1908*

Although the present building is 19th-century, it stands over a Tudor cellar, which clearly indicates that rebuilding took place in the past. The pub used to occupy only a comparatively small corner site but then spread westwards to absorb two neighbouring shops in The Hundred. A careful examination of the decorative brickwork on the upper storey shows clearly that the three houses are not the same although painted the same colour outside and unified inside. Apparently, though, the floor levels are not the same upstairs.

79

This pub was called the *Phoenix* in 1823 when William Woolls was the landlord. The building has clearly been used as a reference point and landmark for many years – as it still is today. In 1846 the Gas Company were planning to lay a gas main from a point near the *Phoenix* to the *William IV* in Latimer Street. In 1859, the proprietor, Mr Cooper, received £5 from the Pavement Commissioners because of the improvement to Latimer Street occasioned by the rebuilding of a wall.

Although Mr Cooper was then the proprietor, his tenant was Robert Fletcher who held the licence for over twenty years. He died in 1880 within a few years of relinquishing the licence. The house was one of the four Romsey pubs that did not become part of the Whitbread empire. It was renamed *The (Romsey) Tavern* towards the end of the 20th century.

## 55    Queens Head, 8 Bell Street **
(see the Royal Oak)

This house changed its name from the *Royal Oak* to the *Queens Head* in the middle of the 19th century. This change may have coincided with the demise of the rather larger coaching inn that had operated in The Hundred as the *Queens Head*. Perhaps the *Royal Oak* hoped to improve its fortunes by taking on the name of a previously more reputable business.

*The old Queens Head, previously the Royal Oak
(in 2006 a long-established antiques shop)*

The Bell Street pub was much smaller than the *Queens Head* in The Hundred, and certainly never achieved the same level of prestige. The pub did not prosper, and lost its licence in 1911. It was by then a common lodging for tramps, and this was felt to be unsuitable for licensed premises. At least twelve tramps had been arrested there in eighteen months. The bar was described as small and cramped. At the time, there were five public houses within forty yards, and this was considered excessive even by Romsey standards.

Aaron Moody was licensee in the 1850s and it is amusing to note that at about the same time a William Moody was the proprietor of a Temperance hotel, also in Bell Street. At the time of the closure, the licensee was Frederick Cook who received £70 compensation. The lessees were the Lion Brewery, Winchester, and they received £409. The owners were only given £241.

It is said that the building dates back to the 17th century. If this is so, it must have been extensively altered in the 20th century.

80

## 56    Queens Head, 7-9 The Hundred **

As a coaching inn, this *Queens Head* was a much grander establishment. The ground floor has been altered into shops but the upper two floors are very little changed externally. Worth noticing are the double sash windows to both the upper floors.

The house clearly reached its heyday at the latter end of the 18th century and the early part of the 19th century. It was fortunate in having a large area at the rear. This was approached through a carriage entrance on the east side, just beyond the small shop of that time.

The Land Tax records show that the *Queens Head* was assessed at £1 1s 0d, but in 1807 it was called a house and the rate was reduced to 18s 6d. It is difficult to explain the reason behind this reduction because the *Queens Head* definitely continued in business for many years after that. The schedule for the 1819 tithe allocation gives the owners as Figes and Longcroft: they were local brewers, and not likely to own the property unless it was continuing as licensed premises.

*The old Queens Head, showing the double sash windows on the upper floors*

Certainly, an advertisement in the *Salisbury & Winchester Journal* on Monday, 2nd April 1838 suggests that the inn was still a thriving concern, even allowing for the gloss put on to encourage a new person to apply for the tenancy.

> To be LET, and entered on immediately, - That old-established and well-accustomed MARKET and COMMERCIAL INN, and TAP, the whole in excellent repair, and replete with every requisite accommodation. The range of superior newly-erected stall stables will admit 40 horses. Capital coach-houses, and a spacious yard. For particulars, apply, by letter, post-paid, to M. Moody, auctioneer, brewer, and victualler's appraiser, Market-place, Romsey.

Mr Alfred Stares, pork butcher of the Corn Market, came to Romsey as a ten year old when his parents took over the *Queens Head*. That must have been in 1843, as Mr Stares died in 1923 at the age of ninety. The last known licensee was James Cribb in 1852. The business was clearly finished by the 1860s when the coaching trade finally faded in the face of the railway challenge. The *Queens Head* was not one of the coaching establishments that managed to diversify or find sufficient local custom.

Memories of this inn lived on, however, into the 20th century. The following appeared in the 'By-Gone Romsey Extra' of *The Romsey Advertiser* dated 28th April 1916.

> The Old *Queens Head* Hotel is now occupied by Mr Light, and the great yard, with its many workshops, for basket-making, was once the hotel stabling. In an old newspaper for 1877 is recorded the death of 'Anne Ford, aged 87, who some fifty years ago was on the staff of the old *Queens Head* in the Hundred'.

The basket works mentioned were still going in the Second World War.

## 57 Railway View, 13 Station Road **

Although the house was called *'Railway View'*, the terrace in which it stands is considerably older than the railway. The house at the western end clearly has a timber-framed core visible along the side wall. The terrace is set at an angle from the present street, and curiously aligned with the back path behind the south side of Station Road. This back path may indicate the line of a footpath that once led through the fields that dominated this area before the arrival of the railway promoted the development of Station Road.

The old Railway View

The earliest evidence of the building as a beer house comes in the latter half of the 19th century, when the owners probably sold beer to satisfy the needs of railway passengers. In 1862, Pavement Commissioners found it necessary to put in order the land in front of the *Railway View* so that the pavement might be extended a few yards towards the Railway Station.

In 1882, the sale of the property was the cause of a great dispute and had to be referred to the Courts for settlement. Mr Henry Thornton bought the property for £380 from William Stone. Only the deposit was paid and then Mr Stone's friends sought to annul the sale on the grounds that he was of unsound mind. They were successful.

By 1898, the house was in the hands of Richard Bowen: later, as manager of the *White Horse*, he became mayor of Romsey throughout the First World War. Mr Bowen advertised the *Railway View* as a family and commercial hotel with good stabling accommodation, posting, etc. and headquarters for the Cyclist Touring Club. The business was finally closed in the 1960s.

## 58 Red Lion, 37 The Hundred *

An early building on the site of the *Red Lion* was apparently destroyed by fire in the early 1700s. Documents of 1727 and 1747 describe the property as 'All that messuage or tenement with the garden or piece or parcel of garden ground thereto belonging on which a house formerly stood which was destroyed by fire together with all edifices walls and buildings thereto belonging ...' It is unclear from this whether the fire related to the part of the site on which the *Red Lion* stood or its adjacent land. Within the period of these documents, however, a witness declaration of 1736 made by a Mrs Anne Fielder refers to the dwelling house of her husband, William Fielder, 'known by the name of the *Red Lyon*': so it was operating as a pub by then.

The next known licensee was Edward Knowles, a victualler who took possession in 1756. By 1776, it was a well-established inn. In that year, when it passed into the ownership of Charles Isdell, brewer, it was known as the '*Red Lyon Inn*', being described as:
> 'All that messuage or tenement commonly called or known by the name or sign of the *Red Lyon Inn* or public house with the Brewhouse Washhouse stable backside yard and garden thereunto belonging and adjoining with their and every of their appurtenances situate lying and being in a certain street called the Hundred ... having a house and garden then or late of Jos Bourne in the occupation of said Chas Isdell on the west side a messuage and garden in the occupation of Mr Wools butcher on the east side ... and having the garden formerly of Mary Harding W late of [blank] King and his wife but then of Jno Fleming on the east side of the other part of the said thereby granted garden, the close called Perriton on the south end and the street on the north end.'

Just one licensee is known for the years following Isdell's purchase; this was John Quinton, whose name was published in a 1784 trade directory.

Charles Isdell went into partnership with Samuel Elliott and Michael Futcher. In 1795, ownership of the *Red Lion* was slightly changed, to be held jointly by Charles Isdell, Samuel Elliott and John Latham who had bought into the partnership after the death of Michael Futcher. In the same year, John Latham, the brewer, bought out the partnership totally with the help of his father. For the next twenty-two years *the Red Lion* was part of the Latham empire.

One early licensee kept hens in the attic, a practice that would not be appreciated by modern health inspectors. From the mid-19th century, the house benefited from having long-term licensees. George Cave, one of the last independent brewers, was at the *Red Lion* for at least twenty years between 1850 and 1870, and probably much longer. Pewter has been found, inscribed *Red Lion Brewery* and bearing the name Cave. In 1870, he was selling beer at 6d to 1s 4d a gallon. Subsequently, during the 20th

83

century, the pub was in the hands of a single family, the Cowards, for fifty-eight years.

One effect of this continuity was that a good deal of the bric-a-brac that would normally be cleared out by new tenants remained at the time of the first edition of this book, when the pub was still open. There was a small collection of china beer mugs stamped VR and some pint glasses stamped GR and ER. There was also an old wine glass. The glass of these vessels was very thick – reminiscent of old railway tea cups. One of the beer glasses had straight almost vertical sides and must have been very heavy and awkward to hold when full.

Another survival, invaluable to the researchers of the 1970s, was an inventory of the possessions in the house dating from 1923. In that year, the *Red Lion* was still lit by gas. There were four iron spittoons in the bar but no ashtrays. The floor had coco mats upon it and the bar counter had a zinc top. There was a five-pull beer engine, which was not fitted and was finally removed in 1949. The beer was still drawn straight from the wood into glasses. What was surprising was how few drinking vessels there were. In pewter they had 1 lip quart, 4 lip quarts, 12 straight pints, 1 half pint and beer and spirit measures. In Ware cups, they had 8 straight pints (four cracked), 2 straight half pints (cracked), 6 lip quarts (3 cracked) and 5 lip pints (1 cracked). In glass, there were 53 stamped handled pints (4 cracked), 34 stamped pints, 30 stamped handled half pints, 19 stamped half pints, 24 Bass glasses, 21 Ale glasses, 13 stem ales, 18 pony tumblers, 7 wines, rummer and grog glasses.

There were fixed benches and a deal form. The smoking room had ten Windsor chairs while the bar parlour boasted a 6ft 6in seat as fixed with hair cushion, and nine Windsor chairs. The wicker easy chair and cushion lived in the kitchen. For the further benefit of patrons, the pub had two sets of dominoes (double and single) and two cribbage boards.

The building itself probably benefited from this continuity. In the 1970s, there were wattle walls covered with canvas; and the beams in the cellar showed holes for wattles to be inserted prior to plastering or daubing. The building was next to the jam factory, which was a Tudor building. When that house was destroyed by fire in the 1970s, it must have been very alarming for the occupants of the *Red Lion*.

There was an outbuilding behind the pub, and this was long a meeting place for Romsonians. LTVAS held a number of early meetings there, and the town band met there for over sixty years. A photo exists of the band in 1860, and the successors of these musicians were still meeting at the *Red Lion* in the 1920s.

*The old Red Lion public house*

The *Red Lion* featured in CAMRA's real ale guide, because casks of beer were racked up in the bar and beer drawn straight from the wood. However, the pub closed in the 1970s, since when it has housed an estate agent.

## 59 ([Old] Rising Sun, Woodley)
*(see the Hunters Inn)*

At the end of the 18th and beginning of the 19th century, this pub was variously known as the *Sun*, the *Old Sun*, the *Rising Sun* or the *Old Rising Sun*. These alternatives did little to stop confusion with the *Sun* at the bottom of Winchester Hill by the Sun Arch railway bridge. Hall and Trodd, the brewers who owned the pub, renamed it the *Hunters Inn* quite early in the 19th century, but this name was not firmly established until about 1900.

## 60 Romsey Arms, Banning Street **

The *Romsey Arms* was probably a beer house, which only took a name late on in life in an attempt at aggrandisement. The house is described as being at the bottom of Banning Street on the south side. This may mean that it was in a still existing continuation of Banning Street south of the By-pass, or it may have been on the south side of one of the many alleys off the main street, which itself runs north-south. (Those courts and alleys were demolished to make way for the Broadwater blocks of flats, built in the 1960s.) The only other slight clue states that it had outside steps to the front door. The last licensee sold beer for some time after 1890, but researchers in the 1970s found that most Romsonians had no memory of the house.

85

## 61 Rose and Crown, 16 Latimer Street **

Back in the 1970s, even older Romsonians seemed unaware that this building had been a pub, although it had only closed in 1911 after more than 130 years of existence. It was in business by 1784.

*The Rose and Crown, 1905*

For many years Thomas Jesser kept the pub - he was certainly there in 1823 and still there in 1836 when he attended the Sessions to give evidence against a prisoner. The accused, James Hiscock was lodging at the *Rose & Crown*, and had been trying to sell stolen wool to a local wool merchant, Stephen Witt, who became suspicious. Thomas Jesser testified that he had loaned Hiscock some sacks, his own being wet, and he told this to Constable Pearce when the latter came to search Hiscock's lodging. William Randall, a farmer of Grafton, Wiltshire, had found 24 fleeces missing from his wool store, and identified the 'wet' sacks as his.

Thomas Jesser may have been one of the Jesser and Cressey brewing family. In 1854 the licence was transferred from him to John Edwards.

When the pub was closed in 1911, it was owned by the Lion Brewery of Winchester. It was fully licensed and not just a beer house. Unfortunately, there were five pubs in Latimer Street from the *Phoenix* on the corner with The Hundred to the *William IV* at the opposite end, and this was considered to be excessive. Two could be spared. At that time the brewery had installed a manager rather than a tenant. He agreed that there was a very small trade but he thought the house would make a good club 'there being none in Romsey' (an incorrect statement). It was claimed that the house was in fine condition.

The licensee, Henry Ader, received £30 compensation, the brewery £238 and the owners of the property £241. The house did not become a club. By the 1970s, it had been a fish and chip shop known as Boddington's for the previous 30 years. The proprietors of that business had cleared the cellar of bottles and other items left by the pub and had more recently installed large glass windows. It was thus difficult to visualise the old *Rose and Crown*.

Later in the 20th century the shop became a very popular centre for the dressmakers of the area under the name of *Thimbles*. When the proprietor of that business retired, however, the shop remained empty for some years.

As the 21st century began and Latimer Street was rejuvenated by new pavements and the opening of a supermarket nearby, developers' attention was drawn to smaller available properties in the street. The old *Rose and Crown* was ripe for a new lease of life.

*The old Rose & Crown in early 2005, with 'Thimbles' façade prior to redevelopment*

## 62 (Royal Oak, 8 Bell Street **)
(see the Queens Head, Bell Street)

The *Royal Oak* was never a very grand place and, despite a name change in the 1850s, had sunk very low by 1911 when it was finally closed. It was in business throughout the 19th century, and was used as a landmark by the Pavement Commissioners. In 1829 they were resolving to repair the pavement in front of Mrs Abraham's house adjoining the *Royal Oak*, and in 1853 it was felt necessary to repair the pavement from the corner of Mrs Courtney's to the corner of the *Royal Oak* in Bell Street.

In 1837, the licensee was a man called Stroud who was fined 40s 0d and costs for breaking the licensing law. Joseph May gave the following evidence at the Sessions:
> 'About six weeks ago I was returning home between 11 and 12 o'clock. I passed the *Royal Oak Inn* again and heard a noise in a back room of the said Inn. I waited outside of the door about quarter of an hour and then went into the house. As I was entering I saw a person of the name of Stroud who said he was the landlord. I saw him draw a quart of beer. There were several persons

87

present who had been playing cards. I saw the cards taken off the table'.

The Joseph May who gave evidence was probably the owner of the Town Mill at the far end of Bell Street.

The *Royal Oak* seems to have changed its name to the *Queens Head* between 1853 and 1857. Perhaps it was a wishful attempt to assume the mantle of the *Queens Head* in The Hundred, which was probably closing at the time after enjoying a rather more illustrious reputation during the height of the coaching trade.

The house was on the north corner of The Cornmarket and was a bookmaker's shop in the 1970s. Subsequently, it became a very popular antique shop.

## 63 Sawyers Arms, 95 The Hundred **
*(see the Catherine Wheel)*

This house was once called the *Catherine Wheel*. As the Catherine wheel was a trade mark of carpenters and joiners, the transition to *Sawyers Arms* may have demonstrated a continuation of association with the woodworkers' trade. In the 1970s, the history of this pub was further complicated by speculation that it may have had an even earlier spell as the *Cartwheel*, known to have been in the vicinity. This idea now seems very unlikely as there is stronger evidence that the *Cartwheel* was demolished to make room for Alma Terrace to the east.

The house is probably over 300 years old and has a timber frame and sideways sash windows like those at the *Bricklayers Arms* in Banning Street. On the tithe map of 1845 the house stands on a plot of land over eleven acres in size. It was then owned by James Pearce and occupied by William Mason. The landholding gradually shrank into a modest walled garden.

*The Sawyers Arms, c1917*
*now a private residence*

Emphasising the early link with carpentry, the back sitting room of the property was once a sawpit. When the town fairs were held in Alma Road, the fair men lodged at the *Sawyers Arms* and at one stage paid 6d for bed and breakfast. Later it was recommended by the Cyclists Touring Club for bed and breakfast.

There is no evidence of brewing on the premises. For over 100 years the *Sawyers Arms* was supplied by beer from Smiths Brewery in Love Lane (see the *Old House at Home*). There used to be a well near the kitchen but eventually the water became cloudy, 'full of microbes' according to the licensee of the time.

The authorities wanted to close the *Sawyers Arms* in 1911. They argued that the house was only 150 yards from the *Sceptre* and 160 yards from the *Kings Head* in one direction and the *Bishop Blaize* in the other. The Police added that the house was badly arranged and inconvenient and they had to complain about music. They agreed, however, that the licence was not infringed. Mr Smith, the owner, said that his was a small brewery supplying only his own house and the *Sawyers Arms*. It would destroy his brewery to lose the *Sawyers Arms* as he could not keep going without it. He claimed that his family had owned the house for over 100 years. In his defence ex-Police Inspector May said he lived near the house and it was well conducted. He always bought his supper beer there.

The appeal was successful and the house stayed open until 1960. Mr Smith retired in 1926, and the house belonged to Strong's for the rest of its working days.

# 64    Sceptre, 57 The Hundred **

*The Sceptre, on right, in its hey-day (now Sceptre House)*

The *Sceptre* only lasted for 100 years from 1871 to 1972. It was the last new pub to be built in the town. The wall of this Victorian corner building has bunches of grapes modelled on it; they look most pleasing when freshly painted.

One source says that the house originally belonged to Jesser and Cressey whose company brewed nearby at The Hundred Brewery. An old photograph, however, shows it as a Barlow's house, and it passed to

89

Brickwoods when that company took over Barlow's Brewery. Brickwoods subsequently became part of the Whitbread Brewery empire, thus bringing the *Sceptre* under the same management as most of the pubs in Romsey. After closing in 1972, the *Sceptre* was for a time used to house staff from the *Potters Heron* pub-hotel at Ampfield [*Corus Hotel* in 2006] on the A3090 to Winchester. Later, it was converted for use as commercial offices.

## 65    Ship, The Hundred [or Latimer Street] **

*The Ship was sited somewhere in this stretch of properties*

In 1830, the *Ship* was listed as a tavern in The Hundred. However, in 1834, the Pavement Commissioners called it a public house in Latimer Street, and reduced the rates from £10 to £8.

## 66 (Spotted Cow, Love Lane)
*(see the Old House at Home)*

This was the town's nickname for the Smith's house in Love Lane, more usually known as the *Old House at Home*. It is said that the name arose because Mr Smith lost a cow, and she was finally found in the bar.

## 67 Spotted Dog**

This house seems to have a long if shadowy history, part of its mystery being its location. In 1792 it called itself an inn but this may have been a flight of fancy describing a modest beer house. A 1911 entry in *The Romsey Advertiser* talks of the transfer of the licence to Ann Kimble the widow of John Kimble.

There is complete silence between these dates apart from one mention in 1800 and that is a back-reference to 1785. It relates that at that time a man named Dickman had worked for five years as a post boy at the *White*

90

*Horse* 'where he received no wages.  When he left he took a public house called the *Spotted Dog* in Romsey Infra at the yearly rent of £5'.  Apart from implying that the pub was located within the then small area of Romsey Infra, this uncorroborated evidence is not very helpful.

Dickman's wife was said to have died during his year there and he went to Alresford as a horse keeper, and was given 1s 0d a week by each of the post boys.  This story is told in the Settlement Certificate, when Dickman was claiming to be supported out of the Romsey rates.

## 68 (Snufftakers Arms, Newton Lane **)
*(see the Newton Arms)*

This was probably a nickname for the *Newton Arms*.  However, there was said to be a second beer house of unknown name in Newton (or Hog) Lane, so the Snufftakers Arms could possibly have been this other house.

## 69 Star, 13 The Horsefair
*(see the Black Swan and the Swan and Dolphin)*

The *Star* began its life as the *Swan and Dolphin*, under which name it can definitely be traced back to the 1790s.   If it also had a prior existence as the *Black Swan*, then the time barriers can be pushed back even further to 1746 at least.  The *Swan and Dolphin* name ceased to exist soon after the pub was sold in 1818 as part of the bankruptcy sales relating to John Latham, brewer.

*The Star in The Horsefair*

In 1820, the tenant was William King, who seems to have moved there from the *Vine* in Cherville Street.   Hall and Co., the brewers who bought the premises in 1818 and renamed the pub as the *Star*, sold it on to Strong and Co. Ltd.  In 1865 Strong's were paying just 10s. 0d. a year for the lease but in 1889 this was increased to £12 a year.

In the 1850s, Thomas Stride was licensee of the *Star*.   He gave up the licence within two months of his wife's death in 1854, and Frederick Cole took over.  First he and then Alfred Cole held the licence there for over thirty years.  Four carriers called weekly: Stares called on Mondays on his way to Southampton and on Tuesdays for Appleshaw; Clark called on Thursdays for Southampton and on Fridays for Wallop.

There may, though, have been a break in the Coles' reign at the pub. In 1875, when the *Star* was sold as part of The Horsefair Brewery sale, it was said to be in the occupation of Mr G. Creed. The property was part leasehold and part freehold as the sales particulars relate.

~~~~~~~

### A FREEHOLD AND LEASEHOLD PUBLIC-HOUSE
Known as 'THE STAR'
Cherville Street, Romsey, containing Bar, Smoking-room, Kitchen and Tap-room, Sitting-room, Bagatelle-room, Scullery; *on the two Upper floors –* Dining-room and eight Bedrooms. *Outside –* Stable yard with gates to street, two 6-stall Stables, with Loft over the whole, large open Cart-shed. Small Garden.
In the occupation of Mr G. Creed.
The house is held on lease from Winchester College for a term of thirty years from November 1st, 1859, at a Quit Rent of 10s per annum. The Yard, with Stabling and Garden, is FREEHOLD.

~~~~~~~

A 'Bagatelle-room' also featured at the *Swan* in the Market Place. Perhaps it was the fashionable attraction of the period.

In 1881, a child fell into a nearby stream and was drowned. The inquest was held at the *Star*, a not infrequent use of nearby inns in earlier centuries.

The corner on which the building stands has seen much alteration over time. In 1822, Mr Hall successfully applied to the Pavement Commissioners for permission to lower the pavement adjoining the yard in Cherville Street so as to admit carriages with greater ease. In the 1960s, the building next to the Star was demolished to allow for road widening. This building had at one time been a beer shop, and later became an off-licence.

Like other pubs, the *Star* has let rooms for meetings at various times in its history. At one time the Freemasons were said to have met there, but they offended public opinion and were obliged to move their meetings to Totton. It is not recorded what their offence was.

## 70 Sun Inn, Winchester Hill

The *Sun* was once known as the *Rising Sun* - not to be confused with the *(Old) Rising Sun* that stood at the top of Winchester Hill and was later renamed the *Hunters Inn*.

In 1792, the *Sun* belonged to Messrs Trodd, maltsters. Although it had been in the hands of the brewing industry at such an early date, licensees did not advertise in the 19th-century directories until 1859, a curious omission.

*The Sun Inn, at the bottom of Winchester Hill*
*It has given its name to the nearby railway bridge, known as the Sun Arch.*

The house looks substantial enough (and needs to be with all the traffic thundering by) but it is of curiously primitive construction. In common with other 18th-century buildings, the house has no damp course; nor has it any proper foundations. The woodwork used in construction was very primitive with the ground floor floorboards resting on split tree trunks themselves resting on the ground. In the 1970s, the wood battens in the walls were described as being 'just as they came off the trees'. Another building - on Winchester Hill - seems to have been constructed by the same builder as it is remarkably similar but that has always been a private house.

The building was once, in fact, two houses with a double door in the centre and two staircases rising up the middle. Below the house was a cellar in which was a well. The entrance to the cellar was not apparent but a subterranean brick archway indicated that the entrance was from outside the building. By the early 21st century, these features had disappeared as a result of a succession of alterations.

In the 1990s the building underwent major changes. Internally, small public rooms were opened up to create one large space. Fireplaces were moved to leave one old brick hearth at the eastern end. A kitchen and surface 'cellars' were built at the rear, and finally, in 1997, a single-storeyed extension was added on to the west providing a 30-seater dining area. This looks out on an enclosed patio and garden.

By 2006, the *Sun Inn* was offering guest accommodation. Four bedrooms (three of them en suite) were available, named The Test, Broadlands, Abbey and Palmerston. Independently owned, the pub prided itself on personal and individual-style service.

## 71 Swan Inn, Market Place **
*(see the White Swan)*

The names *Swan* and *White Swan* alternate throughout 19th-century records but seem to relate to the same building. The evidence for them being the same place is discussed under the *White Swan*.

The *Swan Inn* once belonged to Winchester College, which still holds documents relating to the building: these date back to the 15th century. The earliest document is dated 1477, and includes a memorandum of 'certain stuff for said Inn called the *Swan* in Romsey which Warden delivered to the tenant for his use on date of lease'.

*The Romsey Conservative Working Men's Club previously the Swan Inn*

The tenant in question was Thomas Kokys, and the 'stuff' to be delivered was listed as follows:

'In primis 2 grete whiches [chests] whereof one of them is kerven [curved] and the other serveth to put oats in. Item 11 bedsteads of which 3 are in high turret over great chamber, 2 in chief chamber, 2 in white chamber, 2 in Howell chamber and one in parlour. Item in great chamber is a long board, a pair of trestles and a form. Item in hall is a long shelf board and a bench and a bar of iron in the chimney there. Item in parlour is another bench. Item in kitchen is a dressing board, a bar of iron to hang pots and an old coop. Item in cellar is a board and a pair of trestles. Item 3 stables racked and their mangers. Item said Thomas hath delivered to him by said John 11 doors locked with their keys.'

The next detailed description comes nearly 400 years later, when the *Swan* was sold as one of the assets of The Horsefair Brewery with a rental valuation of £20 a year. This valuation, however, was based on a leasehold corn-rent, a popular way of hedging against inflation as the cost of corn rose and fell.

94

~~~~~~

## A LEASEHOLD PUBLIC-HOUSE
### Known as 'THE SWAN'

Situate in the Market-place, Romsey, and containing – Bar and Bar-parlour, Sitting-room, Tap-room, Bagatelle-room, Kitchen. On the Upper Floors – Sitting-room, 5 Bed-rooms, and 2 Attics. Outside – Store-room, Cellar, Wash-house, a 5-stall Stable, a 2-stall ditto, Cart-shed, large Store-house, and Yard

In the occupation Mr ~~Withers~~ Wise *[altered by hand]*

Held on a lease from Winchester College for a term of 30 years from Michaelmas, 1864, at a corn rent, varying slightly every year, the amount last year being £9 18s. This includes five acres of Land not sold. The sum apportioned on 'The Swan' will be £____ *[annotated by hand 'how much']*

~~~~~~

Apart from the 'Bagatelle-room' the accommodation does not sound as exotic as in 1477, but in essence the building was unchanged in 1875.

At that time, the only structural change known to have been made was to the far west end, where a section had long been leased out as a separate concern. In 1809, when the corner of the building was adapted at the request of the turnpike trustees, the tenant was Aaron Newman, peruke-maker [wig-maker]. The abrupt corner, which had made a very tight turning into Church Street, was rounded off to allow easier access for stage coaches.

A couple of years after the sale of The Horsefair Brewery, it was decided to alter the corner even more drastically. After the introduction of pavements, traffic congestion along Church Street, particularly between the Market Place and Church Place, had become more and more dangerous. At its narrowest, the street was only 13 feet wide including the pavements.

Following the enlargement of the Borough of Romsey in 1876, a newly formed Sanitary Authority determined to widen the whole stretch of Church Street between the Market Place and Church Place. The *Swan's* western building was sacrificed and only survives as a residual, vaguely triangular, shop within Church Street.

The *Swan* and the southern part of the *Falcon* in Church Street both stood on land owned by Winchester College, the back of each site abutting on the other to form an L shape. It is said that at one time they both had the same proprietor, who built an underground passage between the two. The passage no longer exists even if it were ever there.

Over the years, the *Swan* was a good class of hotel and seems to have been more directly involved with Romsey life than the *Bell* or the *White Horse*, which catered predominantly for well-to-do travellers. As an example of this, in 1790 a company of actors, described as playing at the New Theatre, stayed at the *Swan* and were selling tickets there.

There is some confusion about landlords in the 1790s. The Directory of 1792 gives John Ludford as the licensee, but Miss Mary Budden, speaking in 1805, talked of going to work with Mr Taylor at the *Swan* some fourteen years before which would have been 1791. It is probable that Miss Budden was mistaken. John Ludford seems to have moved to the *Swan* from the *Dolphin* where he was proprietor in 1784. Both houses did a similar sort of trade but with the *Swan* perhaps being the grander establishment.

Miss Mary Budden was probably an elderly person by 1805. At that time she was claiming relief out of the Poor Rates, so she may have been very uneducated as well. Her story was that she worked for one year for Thomas Webb, a victualler, at the wage of 1s 0d a week and board and lodging. (He was probably the Thomas Webb at the *Fox Inn*.) Then she went to Mr Taylor on monthly wages entering his service when he went to the *Swan Inn* and leaving him when he left there.

By 1825, Charles Hall was the proprietor and John Gilpin his tenant. In 1826, Charles Hall was both proprietor and tenant. The Land Tax at that time was 10s 10d.

The inn continued to serve the town for many years after this. Private rooms were hired for convivial meetings, where enthusiasts attended for such things as recitals and refreshments. The Oddfellows Lodge met there for over sixty years, and *The Romsey Record* reported in January 1880 that the staff of 'Mr G. Wheeler, Builder, and Mr Marshall, House Decorator', sat down to a workmen's supper. Nearly sixty were served. In May of that year 'Mr Bushman, the spirited host of the *Swan'* catered for the Oddfellows Fete at Broadlands.

The *Swan* ceased being an inn in the 1890s, after which David Faber, of Strong & Co. Ltd, transferred the building to the Working Men's Conservative Association.

The age of the building was appreciated during late-20ᵗʰ-century renovation work, when very old wattle and daub panels were found between old beams; these had been concealed behind more recent wall coverings. Unfortunately, it was not thought possible to retain the old beams, so most of them were removed except in one portion of the roof. New timber was introduced into the refurbished façade together with a heavy oak door frame to the entrance. Unfortunately, a fire in the roof in the late 1970s destroyed the last vestiges of the old inn's original timber framework.

The superb bracket outside the building is very old. It was long thought to have been one from which a soldier was hanged after being found guilty of murder and robbery during the Civil War. Since the 1970s, however, further research has suggested that this particular bracket was probably transferred from the *Bell Inn*: the ironwork features the cut-out of a bell and the initials IH, which could stand for John Hacke, a notable 17ᵗʰ-century innkeeper at the *Bell* (I and J being interchangeable historically).

## 72 (Swan and Dolphin, Cherville Street)
*(See the Black Swan and the Star)*

The earliest discovered reference to the *Swan and Dolphin* is for 1779, when William Galpine insured it with the Royal Exchange Insurance Company. The building, described as brick and tiled, was insured for £400; the furniture therein for £170; the utensils and stock-in-trade for £130; the separate excise office for £30; and a brick and tiled stable for £20. It seems to have been a valuable establishment. After William Galpine's death, his heirs sold the pub to Romsey brewer, John Latham.

The *Swan and Dolphin* may also have had an even earlier spell as the *Black Swan*. A pub of that name existed in 1746, probably in the Horsefair vicinity, but there are no definite links between the two names. The Horsefair was considered to be part of Cherville Street at that time.

The *Swan and Dolphin* name appears in the Land Tax records between 1800 and 1821. In 1812, the tenancy changed from S. Dawkins to William Taylor, and the Land Tax dropped from 17s 2d to 10s 9d.

The pub was sold by auction in 1818 following John Latham's bankruptcy. At the time of the auction the relevant particulars of sale described the pub thus:

> All that respectable and well built inn, called the *Swan and Dolphin*; containing six sleeping rooms, dining or club room with 2 fireplaces, large and small parlours, bar, spacious kitchen, wash house, large underground cellar, and Soldiers apartments, with two stalled stables for ten horses, an open stable for eight, and corn stores over, and the outhouses and yard thereto belonging; situate in the Horse Fair in the town of Romsey in the occupation of Mr William Taylor, as a yearly tenant, at the rent of £15 pa.
>
> These premises have every accommodation for carrying on an extensive business. From its unrivalled situation, it will always command a good trade; and will realize a comfortable income for an active and a respectable family.
>
> The above Inn, and a small part of the yard and outhouses adjoining, are held by lease under the warden and scholars of Winchester College, for a term of forty years, commencing the 1st Nov 1794, at the yearly rent of 10s. The Lease contains covenants, on the lessee's part, to repair the premises, and to pay all quit rents, and other payments and duties issuing out of the premises; and provisos for making the lease void, on assignment thereof, without licence from the lessors; on nonpayment of the rent for thirty days; if the premises should not be repaired, after six months notice; and on nonperformance of the covenants.
>
> The stables and yard adjoining the north side of the above premises, are freehold.
>
> This Lot is subject to a land tax of 10s 9d pa and a quit rent of 5s pa

The pub was bought by Thomas Hall and Charles John Hall, brewers. They renamed it the *Star*, a move that not only marked a new beginning but also saved confusion with two other pubs in the town, namely the *Dolphin* and the *Swan* respectively. By 1822, Hall and Co. were certainly still paying a Land Tax of 10s 10d on the pub but under the name of the *Star*.

NOTE: The *Swan and Dolphin* was recorded as being in Cherville Street, while, rather confusingly, the address of the *Star* is Horsefair. This is because Horsefair is a comparatively modern name, not being found at all until the mid-18th century. Instead the name of Cherville Street was applied much further towards the town centre, reaching as far as the junction of Portersbridge Street with Church Street. At that point a bridge once crossed the waterway that now runs underground, and this made a natural division of streets.

## 73 The Tavern, 32 The Hundred
*(see the Phoenix)*

Since 1974, the pub then known as the *Phoenix* has experienced several name changes. It became successively '*Flames*', *the Romsey Ale-House* and most recently *The Tavern*. The history of this establishment is given under its long-term name of the *Phoenix*.

*The Tavern public house*
*previously the Phoenix*

## 74 Thatched Cottage, Mill Lane **

For many years there was a brewery on this site. It was long in the possession of the Figes family, notably Hatton Figes, senior, and his nephew, Hatton Figes, junior, in the mid-Victorian period.

98

By the 20th century it had become a beer house only, and no longer brewed. It lost its licence in 1918 when the licensee, Edward William Calley, received £80 compensation and Strong's, the owners, received £660.

It is now a private residence, very picturesque with its thatch and visible timbers; it is difficult to see from the road since it is surrounded by a high hedge.

*The Thatched Cottage c 1970s*

# 75    (Three Tuns, Greatbridge)
*(see the Dukes Head)*

*Three Tuns* was just one of a series of comparatively short-lived names for the pub to the north of Romsey long known as the *Dukes Head*.

# 76 Three Tuns, Middlebridge Street

This is another old house, reputed to have been built in the first half of the 17th century. The earliest references to it as a pub, however, only date back to the 1780s, suggesting that it was yet another response to the growing coaching trade. Certainly, it was on the key route into central Romsey for traffic approaching over Middlebridge, but it was not without competition over the years. On the Mainstone side of Middlebridge were the *Horse & Jockey*, the *Lamb* and the *Bridge Tavern*, whilst in Middlebridge Street itself were the *Blacksmiths Arms* and the *Woolpack*. Of them all, however, only the *Three Tuns* survived into the 21st century.

*The Three Tuns, c1970s*

In 1785, the licensee was held up by a highwayman and was so frightened that he had to give up his business. This may have been William Bach, whose name appears as the licensee in a Trade Directory for 1784. The story about the highwayman is likely to be true since it appeared in the *Salisbury Journal* for that year. By 1792, Bach had certainly gone and John Chandler had taken his place.

Many of the 19th-century licensees were farmers, and they sold milk as well as beer. The house seems to have had a long settled period. The Hunt family were there from at least 1823 to 1855. In the 1860s and 1870s Mr and Mrs Rennell were in charge of the business. By 1878, it had passed to James Whitlock and he and Elizabeth Whitlock were there until 1911.

During the 1850s, the carrier Jerred called on Mondays and Fridays on his way to Southampton. The proximity of the *Three Tuns* was one of the reasons given for the closure of the *Woolpack* in 1911. The *Three Tuns* had the local advantage of being a Strong's pub, while the *Woolpack* was a Lion Brewery house, a Winchester-based firm.

The *Three Tuns* was another pub that was sometimes used for holding an inquest. On two occasions at least, in 1866 and again in 1905, the coroner was investigating deaths by drowning. *The Hampshire Advertiser* of 30 June 1866 reported '... the Coroner said he had only recently held an inquest into the death of a child drowned in the same stream. Several jurymen said they had saved children and one tradesman had taken out no less than 67. Verdict: Accidentally drowned. The Jury requested that the Coroner communicate with the Mayor'. This request probably related to the unfenced nature of the stream so close to the first Boys' National School, which was just beyond the *Three Tuns* on the site of Nos 64 and 66. Lord Palmerston had earlier written to the Borough on this very matter.

In 1875, the *Three Tuns* belonged to The Horsefair Brewery. It was then offered for sale as part of that concern.

~~~~~~

A FREEHOLD PUBLIC-HOUSE
Known as 'THE THREE TUNS'
Middlebridge Street, Romsey, containing Bar, Parlour, Tap-room, Cellar &c., three rooms over; 4-stall Stable, &c. In the occupation of Mrs Rennell.
Two Cottages adjoining, each containing three rooms and wash-house.

~~~~~~

Altogether the properties offered under this lot brought in £30 rent a year.

An early photograph of the house shows two small shops adjoining the pub, probably the two cottages advertised in 1875. They were so small that they must have been very modest businesses. Unsurprisingly, they did not last into the modern shopping era, and were absorbed into the pub. In the 1970s the licensee's dog would not go along the corridor into that part of the building.

It is interesting to note that the entrance to the right of the pub building was originally a very historic street, known in medieval times as Eny Street but later down-graded to Eny Lane. This is thought to have been the ancient

100

route out of Romsey towards the New Forest in very early times, before Middlebridge was constructed as a new river crossing (perhaps in the 12$^{th}$ century). It is conjectured that Eny Street led to Waldrons Bridge, which once spanned the Test further south within the present Broadlands Park. This bridge, demolished by the 2$^{nd}$ Lord Palmerston in the 1770s, may once have been the main one on the south side of town. This surviving section of the ancient Eny Street was still being used as a link through from Middlebridge Street to the By-pass as recently as the 1970s, but was closed following an accident to the licensee's small daughter.

The *Three Tuns* pub still has a bow window such as once characterised so many of Romsey's hostelries. It survived the edicts of the 19$^{th}$-century Pavement Commissioners because it was set back behind the Middlebridge Street stream, and therefore did not raise the wrath of that body by impeding the creation of pavements and similar works.

There is no evidence of brewing on the premises, although a convenient stream runs right under the house (as well as the town stream running in front of it). Despite the presence of these streams it was thought that there had been a shallow cellar to the building, but by the 1970s there was no evidence of such. The house has a timber frame that seems stout enough, though it has had to endure flooding at times.

The *Three Tuns* has changed to meet circumstances over the years. As the coaching trade faded, it found favour as a local pub but has recently been renovated for wider appeal as a pub restaurant.

## 77 Tudor Rose, The Cornmarket
*(see the Bugle)*

This modest-looking house has a very long history, though its role as a pub can only be traced back to the 19$^{th}$ century. The building is made of massive oak beams placed close together, as was the style in the 15$^{th}$ century when it was probably constructed.

Upstairs, above the bar, is a half-timbered Tudor Hall of impressive quality. There is a stone fireplace at one end, though it may not have been in this room originally.

Regrettably, because of modern day fire regulations, the room cannot be opened to the public.

*The Tudor Rose, Cornmarket*

101

Evidence suggests that this hall was a high-status meeting place rather than a domestic property. The 15th-century style means that the Guild of St George is a strong contender as builder and first owner. This guild or brotherhood received its charter of incorporation from Edward IV in 1475, and became one of the most successful and apparently the wealthiest of several such guilds in Romsey. It was from the membership of the guilds that the men emerged who eventually formed the nucleus of local civic administration after the dissolution of Romsey Abbey.

There is a considerable lapse of time between the building's suggested use as a guildhall and its life as a licensed house. In the intervening centuries it served many purposes including being the workhouse, a house of Mercy [a refuge or penitentiary] and a brothel.

For many years the age of the building was not realised, and during its earlier years as a public house it was called the *Bugle*. In 1928, however, the building was restored, timbers were exposed, and the partitions that turned the upper hall into a passage and bedrooms were removed.

This revealed the old hall, and the house was renamed the *Tudor Rose*. For many years, Lovibonds of Salisbury owned the pub. They were absorbed by Georges of Bristol, which amalgamated with Courages in 1961. The tenant in the 1970s claimed to have the only pub within Romsey in the Good Beer Guide. This claim was based on the fact that the *Tudor Rose* had a full mention/recommendation.

# 78    Tumbledown Dicks **
(see the Yeoman Public House)

*Tumbledown Dicks* was the town's own name for the beer house on the corner of Love Lane and Latimer Street. Even after rebuilding the name persisted. It may be the same establishment as the *Yeoman Public House*.

*Site of Tumbledown Dicks on corner of Latimer Street and Love Lane*

## 79    Vine, 54 Cherville Street **
*(see the New Inn)*

*The Vine* is another old, timber-framed building with a brick façade and a large bay window that has survived because the property is set back from the street frontage. It was a tied house for a very long time. In the latter decades of the 18<sup>th</sup> century, the King family seems to have established a dynasty that lasted for some fifty years. By 1800, when *The Vine* belonged to Trodd and Hall, the brewers, the tenant was R. King. He had been preceded twenty years earlier by John King, and in 1816 was replaced by William King. William King was the last of the King family at the pub, giving way to a Betteridge in 1822.

A lofty room at the back of the building may once have had a floor put in half way up. With walls being straight for several feet and then arching gracefully to a very small ceiling, the general shape of the room – and one of the upright beams in particular - suggests a late cruck construction of two bays, considerably older than the rest of the property.

The licensees did not always escape the attentions of the law. A serious breach of the licence occurred in 1873. At 11.40pm Constable William Pearce saw William West come out of *The Vine*. He went into the kitchen and saw four people smoking and drinking. Mr Gear, the licensee, said the people had just come in, and William West agreed with this. Furthermore, two of the men were lodgers and Jeremiah Holloway had only come for some greens. The Bench were unable to accept the defence and fined Gear £1 12s 0d, a large sum of money in those days. There is also a brief report in 1917 that Frederick Wheeler was fined 5s 0d for supplying liquor for consumption off the premises after 8pm.

*The old Vine public house now a private residence*

The 1875 sales particulars of The Horsefair Brewery included *The Vine*, stating that it was formerly known as the *New Inn*. The only known reference to a pub of this name is found in Pigot's Directory for 1823. No other information has been found, and lacking further evidence this name has not been given a separate entry.

~~~~~~~

A FREEHOLD PUBLIC-HOUSE
Known as 'THE VINE INN'

103

(Formerly 'THE NEW INN')
Cherville Street, Romsey, containing on the *three Upper floors* –
five Bedrooms; *Ground floor* – Tap-room, Bar, Kitchen, Parlour,
Yard, Wash-house, Cellar, and Stabling for two horses.   In the
occupation of Mr J. Austin.

~~~~~~~

*The Vine* closed as licensed premises around 1970, and became a private
residence.

## 80 Volunteer, Mill Lane **
*(see the Globe)*

The renovated building that
was once the Volunteer public
house

This is a shadowy beer house.
Beyond    knowing    which
building it was, there does not
seem to be any information
about it.  In the 1970s, it was
described as 'the little old
bungalow on the right before
Holman Drive'.  Subsequently,
later in the 20th century, it
was renovated and the area
behind developed to create a little enclave that pleasingly perpetuated the
pub name as Volunteer Yard.

*The Volunteer* probably took its name from the Volunteer Militia, who may
well have frequented it when going to and from the rifle butts beyond the far
end of Mill Lane.

This hostelry may also have been called the *Globe*.

## 81 Wheatsheaf, 103-109 The Hundred *
*(see the Barley Mow)*

One old writer on Romsey said that Alma Terrace (west of the Police Station)
was built upon the ruins of the *The Wheatsheaf* as well as the *Barley Mow*.
It has not been possible to corroborate this assertion and the known deeds
of houses in Alma Terrace refer only to the *Barley Mow*, (otherwise known as
the *Packhorse* or the *Cartwheel*).   Perhaps the *Wheatsheaf* was only a
modest beer house.

## 82 Wheel **

The only reference to this pub comes in the directory of 1784, when Richard
Peters was the proprietor. It may have been related to the *Catherine Wheel*,
one of the pubs called the *Cartwheel* or the *New Wheel* (qv).

## 83 (White Hart, Mainstone or Middlebridge Street) **
*(see the Bridge Tavern)*

Very little is known about this house although licensees of the *White Hart* appear in trade directories of 1784, 1792, 1823 and 1830. It must have been renamed the *Bridge Tavern* sometime between 1830 and 1854, after which licensees appear under the new name. The house is middle-aged by Romsey pub standards and was once owned by the Broadlands Estate.

## 84 White Hart, The Hundred**

Only one reference has been found to this particular *White Hart*, which may have closed by the time the name was being used at Mainstone. In a witness statement of 1736 it was described as an ale-house situated opposite the *Red Lion* and kept by Susanna Fryer and her son-in-law, John Dowden.

## 85 White Horse, 19 Market Place

The *White Horse* has a well-documented history, among the best of any hostelry in Romsey. In the 1970s the inn had the advantage of being under a management that appreciated the oldness of the building. This has not always been the case: the house has undergone various ups and downs, though it is deserving of the highest degree of sympathetic attention.

Despite its Georgian façade, the present building probably dates from the time of Henry VII. Experts consider it to be a high status property, perhaps sponsored by the Abbey. Two long rows of small windows along the side wall on the first and second floors are probably infilling of Tudor open galleries, typical of the sort found on many inns of comparable age and size.

*White Horse Hotel*

There are several Tudor paintings on internal walls of the building. One is of a black Tudor rose linked by a curved geometric design. Another wall painting has also been uncovered and renovated by an expert in the field. Along a beam there is a decoration of Tudor dragons, and this was once part of a larger painting. There is a suggestion that some of the paintings may be covering even older work, which implies that Tudor rebuilding on the site was less comprehensive than usually thought, and that parts of the building may be even older.

It is possible that the *White Horse* began as a guest house for Romsey Abbey in the 12th century. There are early stone cellars, which were renovated in Tudor times, when the bulk of the present building was erected. Successive proprietors have claimed an underground passage, now disused, that once led to Romsey Abbey. This fanciful idea is difficult to believe as a substantial but now hidden stream flows down Church Street between the two buildings.

The name of the *White Horse* is long-established, being found in some early documents. On 1st March 1572, John Uvedale made his nuncupative [spoken] will as he lay sick and dying in a chamber of the *White Horse*. A few decades later and the *White Horse* of Jacobean times is brought to life in the will and inventory of Lucilla Dixson, widow. She died in 1610, leaving the contents of various rooms as bequests. These rooms are named in the inventory as the Hall, Crown Chamber, Great Chamber, Gallerie Chamber, Gallerie Middle Chamber, Gallerie Little Chamber, Parlour, Buttery [store room] and Kitchen. The three 'Gallerie' rooms match well with three rooms that can still be identified today despite later alterations. They are in the range that runs back from the street, where a one-time open gallery is now a closed-in corridor.

Although a solid presence in the town since Tudor times at least, and long an inn of the first importance, the *White Horse* probably reached the height of its commercial significance during the coaching era. Dr John Latham writing around 1810 referred to the *White Horse* in the following terms:
'This town is a leading road to the west and a good thoroughfare with good inns viz the *White Horse* which is the principal one and several others of inferior note, beside which are several public houses, an whole twenty or more in number. In the principal Inn, in course the public is accommodated with post chaises and horses, besides which stage coaches pass daily to London, Portsmouth, Southampton, Salisbury and from the latter to Bath, Bristol and many other places westward.'

In 1776, the *White Horse* had 35 beds, 6 rooms, stabling for 50 horses and room for four carriages. Although the hotel still has many bedrooms, the staff would be embarrassed by the arrival of a single horse nowadays, the livery stables having been adapted for other use. But there is a car park, which in the 1970s had a 'murderously blind exit' into the Market Place. Traffic today is restricted to the rear entrance from Latimer Street.

In 1811, the Pavement Commission paid £3 13s 0d on surveying fees at the *White Horse*. The Commissioners were trying to clear the streets, and pave and light the town. Where they could, they were persuading owners to rebuild their frontages where these jutted out over the footway. They even

106

provided financial help for such work. It may be following this survey that the *White Horse* acquired its early-19th-century façade.

For many years there was a street lamp outside the *White Horse*. In 1829, there were complaints about its not burning at 10 or 11pm in October. In 1841, Robert Cocks was 'allowed £1 per annum for lighting the lamp in front of his house as often as the public lamps are lit'. In 1848, the Pavement Commissioners decided to tell Mrs Cocks the 'the lamp in front of the *White Horse* must be lit according to the original agreement'. There are frequent mentions of the *White Horse* in the records of Romsey. As well as creating a coaching venue for private and public transport, successive managements ensured the durability of the hotel when so many were forced to close after the advent of the railway. This was achieved by diversifying, so that the *White Horse* did not stand or fall solely on the strength of the coaching trade, but also attracted regular local business. At one time there was a cockpit under the room that is the restaurant in 2006. Rather more elegantly, there were Assembly Rooms at the *White Horse*. Perhaps these were in the clapboard-fronted building on the east of the inn yard and facing the side of the main hotel. The hotel was always a popular venue for local events ranging from numerous auctions to grand annual dinners for the more prestigious local societies.

In 1817, the hotel became the centre for hearings of the Bankruptcy order made against the local brewer, John Latham, from whose bankruptcy records so much is learned about the many Romsey pubs within his collapsed empire. Later, there are references to the *White Horse* Market Ordinary in both 1880 and 1881, an 'ordinary' being a good-value basic meal, in this case probably a special offer on market days. The *White Horse* clearly threw its net wide, and thrived when other coaching inns were defeated by competition from the railway.

Needless to say a house of that size required a good number of employees. Inevitably, one or two of the *White Horse's* ex-employees fell upon hard times. John Dickman appeared to claim a Settlement in 1800, and his claim was that about twenty years earlier he had entered into the service of Charles Sibley of the *White Horse* as a post boy: he had stayed for five years. He had received no wages. He subsequently went to the *Spotted Dog* for a year. In 1802, Isaac Newman similarly was claiming relief on the Parish. His claim was based partly on the fact that, in 1787, he was hired to Mrs Sibley at the *White Horse Inn* for £1 10s 0d pa.

By 1878, Vincent Newman was licensee. He died the following year 'under circumstances exciting general sympathy'. In 1881, his five-year-old daughter followed him to the grave. Mrs Newman carried on for a year or two after her husband's death. Only six weeks after the event, she had provided a 'bountiful and satisfying repast' for the Master Builders of Portsmouth in the Orangery at Broadlands.

The *White Horse* was offered for sale in 1848, and the sales particulars provide excellent details of the building at that time, together with a plan of

107

the entire site. The outbuildings at the rear provided two coach-houses and generous stabling as needed for the transport of the day. There was also a brewery, part of which was built over the Holbrook stream and which was set up for a Four-Quarter Plant. Nearby was the *White Horse Tap* for staff and less well-heeled customers.

The *White Horse* changed hands several times during the 20th century, and in 2006 new owners were proposing controversial changes.

## 86 (White Swan, Market Place **)
*(see the Swan)*

There is evidence that this was an alternative name for the *Swan* although the evidence is not conclusive. In 1818, Thomas Vulkis was the innkeeper according to a newspaper report. Five years later, the 1823 Directory named James Gilpin as the proprietor of the *White Swan* and in 1825 John Gilpin was the tenant of the *Swan Inn* or perhaps *Swan Mead*. The Oddfellows were meeting at the *White Swan* in 1821 and at the *Swan* in 1882. On the other hand, the *Swan* was listed as such in 1792 and its 19th-century deeds call it '*Le Swan*'.

Daniel Newman is given as the licensee of the *White Swan* in 1852 but in 1855 Harriet Newman is spoken of as the daughter of Mr D. Newman late of the *Swan Inn*. In 1857 and 1859 Thomas Powell was at the *White Swan* and there are no entries for the *Swan*. Henry Jones was at the *Swan* in 1867, and William Young in 1878. Then, after more than twenty years, there is a final reference to the *White Swan* in 1880, when Henry Fryers was said to be there. The *Swan Inn* closed its doors in 1894.

## 87 William IV, Latimer Street

When this house was rebuilt in 1929, the expense of the work caused the financial collapse of the brewery. Until that time the William IV was the tied house of the Lion Brewery, Winchester. In order to rebuild the house, they sold the adjacent cottages but these did not fetch enough money and the Lion Brewery allowed itself to be bought out by Strong's Brewery.

The old *William IV* was built onto the pavement in line with the adjacent cottages, and had an archway at the side for carts and horses to go through. It seems that it was quite an old building, one clue being that, on entering the front door, customers had to descend two steps. This is an even steeper change of levels than the several Romsey pubs with a single step down.

It is not known how old the previous *William IV* was. The present building has a brick in the wall by the door inscribed MB 1768, which presumably belonged to the old building. On the other side of the door is a brick inscribed 1929, the date of the rebuilding. Nor is it known whether the building had another existence before becoming a pub. Since *William IV* only reigned from 1830 to 1837, the house must have had an earlier name if it were a pub at all before the 1830s; so far licensees have only been identified from 1852 onwards.

There used to be a granary at the back of the pub with wooden pulley blocks *in situ* until about 1970. None of the licensees of the latter half of the 19th century advertised that they were grain merchants so perhaps the property had agricultural use in its earlier years.

*William IV public house*

## 88 Woodmans Arms **
*(see the Mallet and Chisel)*

## 89 Woolpack, 73-77 Middlebridge Street **

This was a very old and rambling house to look at. A photograph taken in 1905 shows a low-set building with a massive central chimney stack and an undulating roof of old clay tiles. The building may have dated from the late 15th or early-16th century.

During the 19th century, the *Woolpack* was in the hands of the Holloway family. The Holloways were brewers and farmers, and Jeremiah John Holloway in 1890 was also a wheelwright. At some stage the Lion Brewery, Winchester, took over the freehold of the place. The Holloways had left by 1905, although one of the family took over the premises of the old *Blacksmiths Arms* for use as a dairy. The last generation of Holloways included twelve children.

The *Woolpack* lost its licence in 1911. Against the house was the fact that it was only 130 yards away from the *Three Tuns*, although this was quite a long way by Romsey standards. The Lion Brewery fought hard to save the licence, arguing that it was one of the oldest houses in Romsey and was in a thoroughfare with a good deal of traffic. There had been no conviction or transfer of licence for five years. The owners claimed to have owned it since 1731, and the deeds certainly went back to that date. In 1900 the Company had spent £220 on the house and stables, and they had plans to spend another £800 on a new building including a tea room. There was stabling for twenty horses, and the yard was big enough for sixty or seventy carts. (Although there was plenty of space behind, it could not have held sixty or seventy carts unless they were stacked vertically!)

The pub ran a club that had thirty-one members, and a petition signed by 130 people was produced. Notwithstanding these arguments, which seem somewhat exaggerated in places, the licence was not renewed. The licensee, who was a manager, received £35 and the Winchester Brewery received £295.

One of the less credible claims argued during the process was that the *Woolpack* was on a main road from Salisbury to the New Forest. Such an argument might have held good before the Southampton to Salisbury Turnpike Trust cut a new connection through Green Hill in the 18th century, but scarcely had much validity in 1911. Even if the petitioners had made a more valid claim regarding the Salisbury to Southampton route, such an argument would have carried less weight than in the days of the coaching trade; in 1911, before the age of the motor car, the railways were dominating travel.

*Woolpack public house, 1905*

According to the deeds, the Winchester Brewery seemed not to have owned the *Woolpack* for anywhere near as long as they had said, though they held documents passed on from previous owners. In fact, Henry Holloway had bought the pub in 1856. It was then mortgaged to Thomas Aylward of Wallop. The Holloways finally redeemed their mortgage to Aylward's executors in 1896. They then took out a new mortgage with Edward Footner and a second mortgage in 1897. It was only in 1900 that they sold the property to the Winchester Brewery.

All appeals having failed, and after a short spell as a private rented property, the *Woolpack* was put up for auction at the *White Horse Hotel* on Thursday, 14th November 1912. The sales particulars for the freehold described it as 'The Quaint Old House for many years past known as The Woolpack Inn'. It was brick-built with a stuccoed front, tiled roof and dormer windows.

On the ground floor, the front room (formerly used as a bar) measured 22ft x 15ft 6in. The living room, also at the front was 15ft x 15ft 3in. Behind and measuring 13ft x 11ft 9in was the back parlour with scullery, washhouse

110

and fuel house beyond. There was also a cellar. Upstairs were five bedrooms, and gas was laid on.

Attached to the house was an old brick and tiled building, formerly used as a brewhouse but then disused. Adjoining this was a brick-built and slated pail closet and urinal plus a timber-built and iron-roofed pail closet. There was also brick-built and slated stabling of recent construction, and this provided a 2-bay open-fronted cart shed and a 4-stall brick-paved stable with large loft over. Next to it, appropriately, was a roomy brick-built manure pit.

There was a spacious yard, enclosed on two sides by corrugated iron fencing, and beyond that a garden 'of productive quality', extending for some 34 rods. The whole property had a street frontage of about 45ft 6in and a total depth of about 260ft. Fortunately, there was a shared right of cartway over a side roadway affording convenient access to the rear of the property.

*Corporation Cottages on site of the Woolpack*

As a selling point the situation was considered to render the site 'a valuable one and highly suited for business premises, especially where spacious yard accommodation would be required, while there is also ample space for the erection of several cottages if desired'. In the event, Romsey Corporation bought the site in 1914 and erected Corporation Cottages.

## 90 Yeoman Public House, Latimer Street **
*(see Tumbledown Dicks)*

This appears in the Pavement Commissioners Records in the following entry for March 1850:
> 'New pavement to be laid in Latimer Street from the corner of the *Yeoman Public House* to termination of buildings connected with *William IV* at the end nearest North Gaston.'

There is no other reference to the *Yeoman* by name. It may have been on the north corner with Love Lane. If so, it was probably another name for the pub that was more commonly called *Tumbledown Dicks* by Romsonians.

## THE PUBLICANS

It has not been possible to compile a complete list of publicans who have played 'mine host' in Romsey pubs over the centuries, but it may be interesting to see those that have been found. The list is given under the names of the pubs in which publicans are known to have served: the date given alongside each name tells the year in which a reference has been found to that particular publican. The Directories have been the main fount of information but they are not wholly reliable. It should be noted that the dates given are simply those on which a licensee was at a given house. It may not be either the beginning or the end of his or her time there. The list gives a clue to the licence holding but no more. Some licensees are omitted altogether and others are probably wrongly named or included after they had left. Nevertheless, the list gives a lot of information about the involvement of certain families, and will help with future research on other buildings. Until the postal service became well established, most houses were referred to by their owners' names and not by their addresses.

NOTES:
**New names**: It has been possible to add quite a few names to this edition.

**+ This plus sign** means that it is not certain that those named were in a given pub. Usually, these doubts relate to beer retailers, though it is likely that they were at a particular named house. In general 20th-century licensees are omitted as are pubs for whom no licensees names have been collected.

**\* This sign** means that the house is still a pub.

| 1 | **Abbey Hotel, \*** |
| | **11 Church Street** |
| 1974 | Eric Ernest Nineham |

| 2 | **Angel,** |
| | **21 Bell Street** |
| 1778 | Stephen Reeves |
| 1782 | John Luter |
| 1784 | Richard Garrett |
| 1792 | William Chalk |
| *1823* | *Joseph Dyett* |
| 1852 | Joseph Webb |
| 1859 | George Mills |
| 1860s | Mr Floyd |
| 1867 | James Reid |
| + | or George Mills |
| 1875 | Mrs Mabbit |
| 1878 | Thomas Mills |
| 1880 | Thomas Mills |
| 1885 | Thomas Mills |

| 1890 | Thomas Mills |
| 1895 | Thomas Mills |
| 1898 | Thomas Mills |
| 1911 | Alfred Andrews, |
| | then Mrs Andrews |
| 1974 | John P. Young |

| 3 | **Barley Mow,** |
| | **103-107 The Hundred** |
| 1851 | Elizabeth Miller |
| 1852 | Elizabeth Miller |
| 1855+ | Elizabeth Miller |
| 1857 | Elizabeth Cole |
| 1859+ | Elizabeth Cole |
| 1869 | Already Closed |

| 4 | **Bell Inn,** |
| | **32 Bell Street** |
| 1667 | John Hack |
| 1667 | Joan Hack |

| | |
|---|---|
| No date | Stephen Spragg |
| 1731 | John Coles |
| 1776 | Jno Faithorn offering post chaise for hire |
| 1784 | John Faithorne |
| 1813 | William Firns |
| 1817 | Mrs Firns |
| 1823 | George Green |
| 1830 | Thomas Travers |
| 1837 | Thomas Travers |
| 1851 | James Riggs |
| 1852 | James Riggs |
| 1859 | James Cribb |
| 1861 | James Cribb |
| 1875 | John Wiltshire Bennett |

**6 Bishop Blaize, * 4 Winchester Road**

| | |
|---|---|
| 1784 | John Jones – and Seedsman |
| 1792 | John Jones |
| 1823 | E. Figgins |
| 1830 | Edw. Halloday |
| 1839 | J. Miller |
| 1852 | Benjamin Stevens |
| 1855 | Benjamin Stevens |
| 1857 | Thomas Higgs |
| 1859 | Thomas Higgs |
| | Thomas Higgins |
| | Mrs Jane Turner |
| 1865 | Alfred Waterman |
| 1867 | George Waterman |
| 1878 | Henry Hitchcock |
| 1880+ | Henry Hitchcock |
| 1885 | William Shove |
| 1890 | William Gayner |
| 1895 | James Pritchard |
| 1898 | James Pritchard |
| 1974 | Brian E. Sizmur |

**7 Blacksmiths Arms, Middlebridge Street**

| | |
|---|---|
| 1855 | Charles Bailey |

**9 Bricklayers Arms, Banning Street**

| | |
|---|---|
| 1830 | Henry Floyd |
| 1867+ | John Edwards |
| 1875+ | Edwards |
| 1878+ | John Edwards |

| | |
|---|---|
| 1880+ | John Edwards |
| 1885 | John Edwards |
| 1890 | John Edwards |
| 1895 | John Edwards |
| 1898 | John Edwards |
| No date | Jess Edwards |
| No date | Mr and Mrs Spencer |
| 1962 | Mr and Mrs Spencer |
| 1973 | Closed |

**10 Bridge Tavern 1 Mainstone**

| | |
|---|---|
| 1854 | John Chandler |
| 1855+ | John Chandler |
| 1857 | John Young |
| 1859+ | John Young |
| 1865+ | John Young |
| 1867+ | John Young |
| 1875+ | Mrs Matilda Young |
| 1878+ | Mrs Matilda Young |
| 1880+ | Mrs Matilda Young |
| 1885+ | John Young |
| 1890 | Albert Drake |
| 1911 | James Stott |
| 1911 | Closed |

**11 Bugle, 3 Cornmarket**

| | |
|---|---|
| 1871 | Mrs Sarah Cole |
| 1875 | William Irvin Bacon |
| 1878 | William Fielder Wilkins |
| 1880 | William Fielder Wilkins |
| 1885 | Thomas Mansbridge |
| 1890 | Thomas Smithers |
| 1895 | John Barfield |
| 1898 | John Barfield |
| 1908 | Jim Dod |

**12 Cartwheel, The Hundred**

| | |
|---|---|
| 1792 | Robert Carter |

**13 Cart Wheel, Newton Lane**

| | |
|---|---|
| 1800 | Nick Slade |
| 1818 | Thomas Purchase |

**14 Cartwheel, Mainstone**

| | |
|---|---|
| 1821 | Thomas Lacey |

113

**15  Catherine Wheel,**
**95 The Hundred**
1792   Robert Carter
1798   Robert Carter
1845   William Mason

**16  Coachmaker's Arms,**
**33 Latimer Street**
1867[+]   Tom Pomeroy
1885[+]   George Edward Lucas
1898[+]   Mrs Caroline Lucas

**17  Compton Arms**
1784   John Jeffery

**19  Cross Keys,**
**11 Bell Street**
1686   John Bingham
1686   Mary Bingham
1784   Edward Moreton
1800   William Moorton
1818   S. Moody
1823   Samuel Moody
1838   Thomas Liddle
1852   William Parks
1855   William Wilkins
1857   William Webb
1859   William Webb
1865   William Webb
1867   George Kendel
1875   Charles Loader
1880   Charles Loader
1885   Frank Hargreaves
1890   Frank Hargreaves
1895   Frank Hargreaves
1972   Closed

**20  Crown,**
**28 The Hundred**
1852   Aaron Moody
1857   Benjamin Stevens
1865   Benjamin Stevens
1867   Benjamin Stevens
1875   St Bungay
1878   James Newman
1880   James Newman
1885   Robert John Fletcher
1890   William Turk
1895   Joseph Henry Argent
1898   Frank Charles Dueli

1970   Closed

**22  Delve Inn,**
**42 Mill Lane**
1852[+]   James Kemish
1855   James Kemish
1857[+]   Daniel Kemish
1880[+]   Josiah Munday
1885[+]   Josiah Munday
1890[+]   Josiah Munday
1898[+]   Josiah Munday
1911   Frederick Wheeler
1911   Closed

**23  Dog,**
**68 Cherville Street**
1800   J. Trandall
1803   S. Moody

**24  Dog and Star**
**68 Cherville Street**
1743   Ambrose Walden
1753   George Warden, younger
1784   Thomas May

**25  Dolphin,**
**9 Corn Market**
1784   John Ludford
1792   John Young – and
        auctioneer
1803   John Young
1817   Mr Self
1823   Stephen Leach
1826   Thomas Figes
1827   Thomas Figes
1828   Thomas Figes
1830   Hatton Figes
1852   William Brown
1854   William Brown
        James Macrow
1856   Watts
1857   Joseph Watts
1859   Thomas Higgs
        Joseph Watts
1865   Mrs Mary Ann Cole
1867   Mrs Mary Ann Cole
1875   Burges Edmunds
1878   John Edwards
1880   John Edwards
1885   John Edwards

114

| 1890 | John Edwards |
| 1898 | John Edwards |
| 1974 | Leslie G. Crowhurst |
| | and Francesco Ruffoni |

**27    Dukes Head, ***
**Greatbridge**

| 1784 | Edward Bare |
| 1800 | James Norris |
| 1828 | James Norris |
| 1855 | George Neil |
| 1857 | George Neil |
| 1859 | George Neil |
| 1885 | John Eldridge |
| 1890 | Henry Tozer |
| 1895 | George Sadlem |
| 1974 | Les Hooper |

**28    Falcon Inn,**
**11 Church Street**

| 1665 | William Ireland |
| 1699 | Roger Buckle |
| 1753 | Alexander Oram |
| 1781 | James Bishop |
| 1784 | James Bishop |
| 1823 | William Lawes |
| 1852 | Thomas Reeves |
| 1855 | James Cribb |
| 1857 | James Cribb |
| 1859 | William Quarterman |

**29    Fleming Arms,**
**Station Road**

| 1875 | James Feltham |
| 1878 | James Feltham |
| 1879 | James Feltham |
| 1880 | James Feltham |
| 1890 | Thomas Loney |
| 1894 | R. Bowen |
| 1895 | Richard Bowen |
| 1918 | Arthur Fuller Wells |
| | Joseph Graham |
| 1974 | H. Bridge |

**30    Flower de Luce**
**or Fleur de Lis**

| 1784 | Mrs Hodges |
| 1823 | James Moore |

**31    Fox Inn,**
**Old Southampton Rd**

| 1784 | Thomas Webb |
| 1792 | Charles Waller |
| 1823 | *James* Judd |
| 1834 | Mrs Judd |
| 1851 | John P. Young |
| 1852 | John Pester Young |
| 1855 | Thomas Charles Jesser |
| 1857 | Thomas Charles Jesser |
| 1859 | Thomas Charles Jesser |
| 1863 | Already Closed |

**32    Globe**

| 1850s | Mr Floyd |

**35    Hatchet**

| 1686 | William Ives |

**36    Horse and Jockey,**
**23 Mainstone**

| Before | |
| 1760 | Mary Bedford |
| 1830 | William Fry |
| 1838 | Richard Cole |
| 1857 | George Edsall |
| 1859 | George Edsall |
| 1878 | Tom Webb |
| 1880 | John Matthews |
| 1885 | John Matthews |
| 1895 | George Townsend |
| 1898 | Charles Robert Payne |
| 1972 | Closed |

**37    Hunters Inn, ***
**Woodley**

| 1792 | William Dunning |
| 1855 | John Chappelow |
| 1857 | John Chappelow |
| 1859 | Charles Philpott |
| 1867 | John Gunnell |
| 1875 | George Parker |
| 1878 | George Parker |
| 1880 | George Parker |
| 1885 | Mrs Ann Parker |
| 1890 | John Weston |
| 1895 | Charles Weston |
| 1898 | Mrs Elsie Weston |
| 1974 | Cecil Thomas Callen |

115

| 38 | Kings Head, 80 The Hundred |
|---|---|
| 1784 | William Wools |
| 1806 | Richard Jeffrey |
| 1823 | Richard Jeffrey |
| 1839 | Richard Jeffrey |
| 1842 | James Cole |
| 1851 | Henry Cole |
| 1852 | Henry Cole |
| 1855 | Henry Cole |
| 1857 | Mary Ann Cole |
| 1867 | John Ridgeley |
| 1878 | James Joseph Talbot |
| 1880 | James Joseph Talbot |
| 1883 | James Joseph Talbot |
| 1885 | Matilda Talbot |
| 1895 | John Simmons |
| 1898 | John Simmons |
| 1974 | Robert Coombs |

| 40 | Lamb Inn, 7 Mainstone |
|---|---|
| 1755 | Richard Crafts |
| 1778 | William Pitters |
| 1784 | George Holloway |
| 1792 | Thomas Slade |
| 1795 | John Pitter |
| | William Winn |
| 1819 | John Collins |
| 1823 | William Bone |
| 1830 | William Salter |
| 1852 | John Tarver |
| 1956+ | Samuel Moody |
| 1857 | Samuel Moody |
| 1859 | Samuel Moody |
| 1883 | Alfred Baker |

| 41 | Lansdowne Arms, 28 & 30 Church St |
|---|---|
| 1852+ | William George Lawes |
| 1855+ | William George Lawes |
| + | Henry Hunt |
| 1857+ | Sarah Hunt |
| 1859+ | Sarah Hunt |
| 1898+ | George Bundy Junior |
| 1911 | Mrs Cicely Simmons |
| 1911 | Closed |

| 42 | Latimer Arms, 11 Latimer Street |
|---|---|
| 1878 | Edward Stares |
| 1885 | Mrs Louisa Stares |
| 1898 | Charles Downing |
| 1916 | Frederick James Latimer |
| 1972 | Closed |

| 44 | Lord Nelson, 68 Cherville Street |
|---|---|
| 1743 | Ambrose Walden |
| 1806 | S. Moody |
| 1809 | S. Moody |
| 1810 | Murrant |
| 1811 | William Stockwell |
| 1812 | John Batten |
| 1813 | Fryer |
| 1815 | Coggins |
| 1816 | Mrs Chandler |
| 1817 | King |
| 1819 | G. Holloway |
| 1820 | G. Medley |
| 1821 | G. Medley |
| 1822 | William Drew |
| 1823 | Josiah Waldron/*Walden* |
| 1824 | J. Miller |
| 1827 | J. Miller |
| 1829 | James Gear |
| 1830 | John Miller |
| 1831 | James Gear |
| 1855+ | James Gear |
| 1875 | W. Landall |

| 47 | Market Inn, 11 Church Street |
|---|---|
| 1855 | Henry Wheeler |
| | Robert Floyd |
| 1867 | George Thomas Russell |
| 1875 | J. Scorey |
| 1878 | John Scorey |
| 1885 | John Scorey |
| 1890 | John Scorey |
| 1895 | John Scorey |

| 49 | Newton Arms, 4 Newton Lane |
|---|---|
| 1890+ | Robert Cole |
| 1898+ | Robert Cole |
| 1917 | Martha Elizabeth Cole |
| 1918 | Closed |

| 49 | **New Wheel** |
|---|---|
| 1823 | J. Waterman |

| 51 | **Old House at Home, Crampmoor** |
|---|---|
| 1859+ | Emos Laurence |
| 1936 | Closed Previously |

| 52 | **Old House at Home, * Love Lane** |
|---|---|
| 1855+ | James Smith |
| 1859+ | James Smith |
| 1875+ | Mrs Rachel Smith |
| 1878+ | Mrs Rachel Smith |
| 1880+ | Mrs Rachel Smith & Sons |
| 1885+ | Thomas Smith |
| 1890+ | Thomas Smith |
| 1898+ | Thomas Smith & James Smith |
| 1974 | Barrie Cook |

| 53 | **Packhorse, The Hundred** |
|---|---|
| 1839 | Robert Cole |

| 54 | **Phoenix, 32 The Hundred** |
|---|---|
| 1795 | John Beavis |
| 1823 | William Woolls |
| 1830 | Sarah Wools |
| 1852 | William Wilkins |
| 1855 | Robert Fletcher |
| 1859 | Robert Fletcher |
| 1867 | Robert Fletcher |
| 1875 | Robert Fletcher |
| 1878 | Robert Fletcher |
| 1880 | Henry Wilson |
| 1883 | Alfred Wareham |
| 1885 | William Ball |
| 1895 | Joseph Hodges |
| 1898 | Frederick George Gray |
| 1974 | H.G. Egerton |

| 55 | **Queens Head, 8 Bell Street** |
|---|---|
| 1855 | Aaron Moody |
| 1857 | Aaron Moody |
| 1859 | Aaron Moody |
| 1867 | Thomas Cole |
| 1875+ | Thomas Williams |

| | |
|---|---|
| 1885+ | Charles Daniel Williams |
| 1895+ | Charles David Williams |
| 1898 | Charles David Williams |
| 1911 | Frederick Cook |
| 1911 | Closed |

| 56 | **Queens Head, 7-9 The Hundred** |
|---|---|
| 1784 | Thomas Meradeth |
| 1792 | George Dawkins |
| 1800 | G. Dawkins |
| 1803 | M. White |
| 1804 | M. Isdell |
| 1805 | M. Isdell |
| 1823 | William Adams |
| 1830 | James Nurse |
| 1843 | Stares |
| 1852 | James Cribb |

| 57 | **Railway View, 13 Station Road** |
|---|---|
| 1885 | George Thomas Russell |
| 1898 | Richard Bowen |
| 1898+ | Edward Noble |

| 58 | **Red Lion, 37 The Hundred** |
|---|---|
| 1736 | William Fielder |
| 1756 | Edward Knowles |
| 1779 | George Newman |
| 1784 | John Quinton |
| 1792 | John Smith |
| 1794 | John Fryer |
| 1795 | Joshua Smith |
| 1819 | Widow (Ann) Fryer |
| 1820 | Joshua Smith |
| 1830 | Sarah Halloday |
| 1850 | George Cave |
| 1852 | George Cave |
| 1855 | George Cave |
| 1859 | George Cave |
| 1867 | George Cave |
| 1870 | George Cave |
| 1875 | George Cave |
| 1878 | George Harnatt |
| 1880 | George Honnatt |
| 1885 | William Springford |
| 1890 | William White |
| 1895 | Root Lillington |
| 1898 | William Blay |

117

| 1916 | Bowers |
| 1916 | Coward Family |
| 1974 | Mrs Florence Coward |

**61 Rose and Crown, Latimer Street**

| 1780 | William Prangnell |
| 1784 | William Plannel |
| 1819 | James Perry or Swift |
| 1823 | Thomas Jesser |
| 1854 | John Edwards |
| 1855+ | John Edwards |
| 1859 | John Edwards |
| 1859 | Mrs Martha Edwards |
| 1885 | William Burnage |
| 190 | Arthur Scorey |
| 1895+ | William Reeves |
| 1898 | William Henry Steele |
| 1911 | Henry Alder |
| 1911 | Closed |

**62 Royal Oak, 8 Bell Street**

| *1823* | *James Jackman* |
| 1823 | Thomas Jackman |
| 1830 | William Mason |
| 1837 | Stroud |
| 1852 | John Reeves |

**63 Sawyers Arms, 95 The Hundred**

| 1884 | George Putname |
| 1885+ | George Putnam |
| 1890 | William Burnett |
| 1898+ | Tom Archer |
| 1903 | Tom Archer |
| 1911 | George Allen |
| 1920s | Charles Bartram |
| 1957 | Kath Bartram |
| 1960 | Closed |

**64 Sceptre, 57 The Hundred**

| 1878+ | John Evans |
| 1884 | John Evans |
| 1891 | John Evans |
| 1898+ | John Evans |
| 1972 | Closed |

**65 Ship, The Hundred (or Latimer Street)**

| 1823 | Ann Ward |
| 1830 | Ann Ward |

**67 Spotted Dog**

| 1785 | Dickman |
| 1792 | William Trendall |
| 1911 | John Kimble |
| | Ann Kimble |

**69 Star, * 13, Horsefair**

| 1821 | W. King |
| 1823 | William King |
| 1830 | Thomas Major |
| 1852 | Thomas Stride |
| 1854 | Thomas Stride |
| 1855 | Frederick Coles |
| 1857 | Frederick Coles |
| 1859 | Frederick Coles |
| 1859 | Frederick Coles |
| 1875 | G. Creed |
| 1878 | Alfred Cole |
| 1880 | Alfred Cole |
| 1885 | Robert Gaymer |
| 1890 | Henry Tibble |
| 1895 | Henry Tibble |
| 1974 | Cecil D. Vane |

**70 Sun Inn, * Winchester Hill**

| 1859 | James Shepherd |
| 1875 | James Shepherd |
| 1878 | James Shepherd |
| 1880 | James Shepherd |
| 1885 | James Shepherd |
| 1895 | John Morrant |
| 1898 | John Morrant |
| 1974 | A. Ostler |

**71 Swan Inn, 13 Market Place**

| 1477 | Thomas Kokys |
| 1743 | ?Matthew Waldron?? |
| 1786 | Taylor |
| 1792 | John Ludford |
| 1825 | John Gilpin |
| 1826 | Charles Hall |

118

| | |
|---|---|
| 1827 | Charles Hall |
| 1841+ | Daniel Newman |
| 1855 | Daniel Newman |
| 1867 | Henry Jones |
| 1878 | William Young |
| 1882 | Parmiter Bushman |
| 1890 | John Scorey |
| 1895 | John Scorey |

**72 Swan & Dolphin,**
**Cherville Street**

| | |
|---|---|
| 1779 | William Galpine |
| 1784 | William Galpin - excise officer |
| 1800 | T. Hardy |
| 1803 | John Dawkins |
| 1805 | S. Dawkins |
| 1811 | S. Dawkins |
| 1812 | William Taylor |
| 1820 | William Taylor |

**74 Thatched Cottage,**
**Mill Lane**

| | |
|---|---|
| 1852 | Hatton Figes (possibly) |
| 1855 | Hatton Figes (possibly) |
| 1918 | Edward William Calley |
| 1918 | Closed |

**76 Three Tuns, ***
**58 Middlebridge St**

| | |
|---|---|
| 1784 | William Bach |
| 1792 | John Chandler |
| 1823 | Richard Hunt |
| 1852 | Richard Hunt |
| 1855 | Charles Hunt |
| 1857 | George Leverton |
| 1859 | George Leverton |
| 1867 | William Rennall |
| 1875 | Mrs Elizabeth Rennall |
| 1878 | James Whitlock |
| 1880 | James Whitlock |
| 1885 | James Whitlock |
| 1890 | James Whitlock |
| 1895 | James Whitlock |
| 1911 | James Whitlock |
| 1911 | William Piper |
| 1974 | David T. Mabey |

**77 Tudor Rose ***
**3 The Corn Market**

| | |
|---|---|
| 1974 | Joseph R. Blincoe |

**79 Vine,**
**54 Cherville Street**

| | |
|---|---|
| 1779 | Edw. Figes |
| 1782 | William Sonnate |
| 1784 | John King |
| 1792 | John King |
| 1800 | R. King |
| 1803 | R. King |
| 1816 | William King |
| 1820 | William King |
| 1822 | Betteridge |
| 1823 | James Betteridge |
| 1825 | Betteridge |
| 1827 | Betteridge |
| 1859 | Harry Carter |
| 1865 | James Cribb |
| 1873 | Mr Gear |
| 1875 | Mark Elliot/J.Austin |
| 1880 | George Whale |
| 1885 | George Whale |
| 1890 | Joseph Thorne |
| 1895 | James Sillence |
| 1898 | James Sillence |
| 1911 | William Piper |
| Approx. 1970 | Closed |

**82 Wheel**

| | |
|---|---|
| 1784 | Richard Peters |

**83 White Hart,**
**1 Mainstone**

| | |
|---|---|
| 1784 | Benjamin Sillence |
| 1792 | Thomas Webb |
| 1823 | John Coggins |
| 1830 | *Thomas Jackman* |

**85 White Horse, ***
**19 Market Place**

| | |
|---|---|
| 1714 | William Freeman, senior |
| 1777 | Charles Sibley |
| 1784 | Charles Sibley |
| 1792 | John Quinton |
| 1823 | James/Jos. Phillips |
| 1830 | Sarah Bell |
| 1841 | Robert Cocks |

119

| 1851 | Mrs Cocks |
| 1855 | Mrs Sarah Cocks |
| 1857 | Mrs Sarah Cocks |
| 1859 | Mrs Sarah Cocks |
| 1865 | Mrs Sarah Cocks |
|  | Mr John Allsop |
| 1867 | Charles Robert Prangnell |
| 1875 | Charles Robert Prangnell |
| 1878 | Vincent Newman |
| 1879 | Vincent Newman |
| 1880 | Richard Talmy-Turner |
| 1885 | Richard Talmy-Turner |
| 1890 | James Bignal |
| 1895 | James Bignal |
| 1898 | James Bignal |
| 1974 | G.J. Edmond and |
|  | M.D. Panni |

**86**  **White Swan,**
**13 Market Place**

| 1818 | Thomas Vulkis |
| 1823 | James Gilpin |
| 1830 | Josiah Gilpin |
| 1852 | Daniel Newman |
| 1857 | Thomas Powell |
| 1880 | Henry Fryers |

**87**  **William IV, ***
**45 Latimer Street**

| 1852 | James Vanderplank |
| 1855 | William Burnage |
| 1857 | William Burnage |
| 1859 | William Burnage |
| 1865 | William Burnage |
| 1867 | William Burnage |
| 1875 | Mrs Mary Burnage |
| 1885 | Mrs Mary Burnage |
| 1890 | Mary Burnage |
| 1895 | Henry Walter Brown |
| 1898 | Henry Walter Brown |
| 1974 | S.G. Parker |

**89**  **Woolpack,**
**73-77 Middlebridge St**

| 1857+ | Henry Holloway |
| 1859+ | Henry Holloway |
| 1875+ | Mrs Elizabeth Holloway |
| 1878+ | Mrs Elizabeth Holloway |
| 1880+ | Mrs Elizabeth Holloway |
| 1885+ | Mrs Elizabeth Holloway |
| 1898+ | Jeremiah John Holloway |
| 1911+ | Edwin Joseph Webb |
| 1911 | Closed |

~~~~~~~~~~~~~~~~~

In addition to the foregoing publicans of named houses, there are a considerable number of other beer retailers. These people are listed by street but not by house number or name, so it is not possible to give their exact place of business. Many of them probably carried on their trade in the houses that were named at other periods of time. However, there is insufficient evidence to place them exactly. Where they give other trades, these are listed below as it may in the future help to locate them.

**Banning Street**
**1852**
John Alexander
James Barnes
Joseph Floyd
William Carden

**1855**
Diane Alexander
William Carden

**1857**
William Carden

Joseph Southwell – Furniture
Broker

**1859**
William Budden
William Carden
Joseph Southwell

**1867**
John Edwards

**1878**
Joseph Marsh

120

**1885**
Frank Leonard Watts

**1890**
Frank Leonard Watts

**Bell Street**
**1852**
William Savage

**1855**
John Hill – Horse Breaker

**1857**
P. Tanner

**1867**
Faithful George, Coffee House

**1878**
Alexander Kemish

**1880**
George Knowlton

**Cherville Street**
**1852**
George Southwell
Thomas Phillips

**1855**
George Chandler
Thomas Phillips

**1857**
George Chandler
Thomas Phillips

**1859**
George Chandler
William Lowe
Thomas Phillips

**1865**
George Chandler
Thomas Stares

**1867**
George Chandler

**1875**
Mrs Sara Chandler – Brewer
William Landall

**1878**
Mrs Sarah Brown
Mrs Sara Chandler
George Whale

**1880**
Edward West

**1885**
George Bundy
George Edmund Sawyer – Mineral
                Water Manufacturer

**Church Lane**
**1859**
George Cooper

**Church Street**
**1859**
George Pearce

**1867**
William Hedditch
William Slater

**1878**
George Reeves – Baker and
                Greengrocer

**1880**
George Reeves – Baker

**1885**
Henry Tibble

**Churchyard**
**1875**
Josiah Munday

**1878**
Josiah Munday

**Cornmarket**
**(formerly Pig Market)**
**1852**
William Legg

**1859**
Henry Wheeler

**1885**
Thomas Mansbridge – Blacksmith

**Cupernham**
**1855**
James Shepherd

**1859**
James Shepherd

**1865**
Henry Webb – Grocer

**1867**
James Shepherd

**Horsefair**
**1855**
John Prince – Brewer

**1859**
Dan Hernish
John Prince – Brewer
Thomas Strong – Brewer
Wiles – Brewer

**The Hundred**
**1839**
W. Mason – Glass and China
                                    Dealer
A. Saint
C. Waterman

**1852**
Mary Casse
John Robert S. Hudson
Sarah Jesser – Brewer
William King
Mary Mason
James Pearce
James Smith
James Stares
George Withers

**1855**
John Gue

Mrs Sarah Jesser – Maltster and
                              Coal Merchant
James Pearce - Grocer
Henry Holloway
Christopher Westbrook

**1859**
James Barnes
Thomas Charles Jesser
John Stone

**1865**
John Stone

**1867**
John Stone
Walter Westbrook

**1875**
Edward Stares – Brewer
James Withers

**1878**
George Carr
James Withers

**1880**
James Withers

**1890**
John Goodridge

**1895**
John Emery

**Love Lane**
**1855**
William Webb

**1859**
Henry Wheeler

**Mainstone**
**1820**
William Webb

**1875**
Joseph Carpenter

122

**1885**
Alfred Baker

**1895**
Fred King

**1898**
Herbert Anthony Brown

**Market Place**
**1855**
Robert Floyd
Henry Wheeler

**1857**
William Overbury Purchase –
    Maltster, Hop Factor and Grocer
Henry Wheeler

**1859**
W.O. Purchase

**1867**
W.O. Purchase

**1878**
W.O. Purchase

**1885**
Charles Medley, Junior

**Middlebridge Street**
**1837**
John Webb

**1852**
Robert Floyd
William Quarterman
Peter Tanner
John Webb
Richard Pearce

**1855**
Job Moody
William Quarterman
John Webb – Brewer

**1857**
James Hogarth – Joiner
Quarterman

**1859**
Mrs Mary Barley – Grocer
Mrs Ellen Alicia Barker
William Fanstone
James Hogarth
James Long
James Webb – Brewer

**1867**
Charles Fripp
Frederick Newman – Brewer

**1875**
Charles Halsted – Shoeing Smith

**1878**
Henry Coc
George Paull

**1885**
Charles Gordon

**1890**
Thomas Mansbridge – Blacksmith

**Mill Lane**
**1857**
Thomas Iremonger

**1859**
James Russell

**1867**
James Russell

**1885**
Alfred Taylor

**1890**
Harry Bettridge

**1895**
Harry Bettridge

**1898**
George Marshall

**Newton Lane (or Hog Lane)**
**1852**
John Holley

**1855**
John Holby

**1857**
John Holby

**1859**
John Holby

**1867**
William Merrick

**1885**
Mrs Caroline Merrick
Henry Baldwin

**1890**
Henry Long

**Palmerston Street**
**(or Southampton Road)**
**1875**
John Evans

**1880**
John Evans – Carpenter

**1885**
John Evans – Carpenter

**1890**
John Evans – Carpenter

**1895**
John Evans – Carpenter

**Station Road**
**1875**

Henry Thornton
**1878**
Henry Thornton

**1880**
Henry Thornton

**1885**
Henry Thornton

**1890**
Henry Thornton

**1895**
H. Thornton

**Winchester Road**
**1859**
John Curtis

**1867**
John Carr
John Curtis

**1878**
Mrs Emily Cressey – Brewer,
Maltster and Spirit Dealer

Winchester Street
1859
Mary Gue

**1875**
George Bungley

**1880**
Cornelius Webb

~~~~~~~~~~~~~~~~

In addition the following licensees are given without any location at all.

**1635**
Richard Symes

**1666**
Thomas Chalke

**1685**
Laurence Watts

**1689**
Alexander Gasse

**1699**
Roger Buckle

**1710**
Elizabeth White, widow (R.Infra)

124

**1713**
Arthur Candy

**1722**
Simon Young (Ranville Common)

**1731**
Thomas Hall

**1764**
Edward Jeffery

**1772**
Thomas Dixon

**1774**
Edward Newman

**1781**
John Floyd (Romsey Infra)

**1792**
Richard Faraday
Thomas Withers

**1796**
William Purchase

**1831**
John Bell

**1836**
William Jeffery

**1841**
Publicans:   Henry Cailes
             Samuel Moody
Innkeepers: James Duke
             Joseph Dyatt
             James Gibbs
             Isaac Hawkin
             William Legge
             Bernard Lintott
             George and John
                         Prince
             Thomas Register
             Thomas Travers
             Robert Tuner
Beer Shop:   Charles Waterman

**1851**
Innkeepers: John Alexander
             William Bourne
             Henry Fish
             Thomas Phillips
             Thomas Taylor
             John Witt

# LIST OF WRITTEN AND PRINTED SOURCES

## Printed Sources

1   Romsey Register – Romsey's local paper during the 19th century
2   Romsey Advertiser – Romsey's local paper in the 20th century
3   Of Personalities and Progress 1858-1969. Edited by Alfred Rose, Published by Strong and Co. of Romsey Limited
4   Romsey Abbey by Charles Spence. Published by C.L. Lordan probably 1870-1880
5   P.O. and similar Directories. A large number of these were consulted. They are found in reference libraries and in the Archives Offices in Winchester and Southampton
6   The Brewing Industry in England 1700-1830 by Peter Mathias
7   A History of the English Public House by H.A. Moncton, published by The Body Head
8   *So Drunk He Must Have Been To Romsey (LTVAS, 1974 edition)*

## Handwritten Sources

1   *Land Tax records 1800-1830,* Hampshire Record Office
2   *Settlement Certificates 1791-1808,* Romsey Town Council 1974
3   *Romsey Sessions Records 1820-1836,* Romsey Town Council 1974
4   *Book of Proceedings of Romsey Pavement Commissioners 1810-1876,* Romsey Town Council 1974
5   Deeds of various houses in possession of Whitbread (Wessex), Romsey Town Council, Romsey Conservative Association and Hampshire Archives Office, Winchester
6   *Latham Mss Notes for the History of Romsey compiled c1810,* British Library Add Mss 26774-267780
7   *Winchester College Muniments, Vol II,* edited by Sheila Himsworth
8   *Royal Exchange Insurance Records,* Guildhall Library (MS Ref: 7253/3-11)
9   *Assorted LTVAS resources*

## The LTVAS Group

The LTVAS Group was founded in 1973 with the objects of excavating sites of archaeological interest; fostering practical interest in, and appreciation of archaeology; recording and surveying the area as existing from the archaeological viewpoint; and researching, collecting and publishing historical records of the Lower Test Valley

If you wish to know more of their work, please contact The LTVAS Chairman, c/o Romsey Town Hall, Market Place, Romsey.

## 'OLD MONEY'

The 1974 edition of this book was published within a couple of years of the country 'going metric'. The first readers were still very familiar with the old imperial currency, and indeed still tended to convert new prices into old money as a precautionary cross-check on possibly inflated charges. In 2006, however, the situation is very different. It was felt that a brief guide of the old monetary system might be useful. Accordingly, a page based on information compiled for the LTVAS 'Millennium' publication, *The History of Romsey*, is reproduced here.

### A GUIDE TO MONEY as used before 1971

**£ s. d.**

Old money, as opposed to the present metric system of money, was most popularly referred to as 'Pounds, shillings and pence'.

- **Pounds**, as now, were identified by the £ sign. This sign comes from a capital L with a line struck through thus £ to show that it is an abbreviation for *Libra*, Latin for a pound.
- **Shillings** were abbreviated as 's.', though this actually came from *solidus*, the Latin for shilling.
- **Pence** were shown as 'd.' from the Latin for a penny, which was *denarius*.

**Pennies**

    12d. = 1 shilling

    240d. = £1

- **Half-penny**: A penny could be divided into halves, each known as a half-penny or ha'penny (½d.)
- **Farthing**: A penny could also be divided into quarters, each known as a farthing (¼d.); three farthings would be represented as ¾d.

**Shillings**

    20s. = £1

    21s. = 1 guinea (£1 1s. 0d.)

    42s. = 2 guineas (£2 2s. 0d.) and so forth

**NOTE**: Sums of shillings and pence might be written as 2s. 6d. or 2/6. The latter style was particularly popular in shop displays: it has been used in this book when part of a quotation.

### Some equivalent sums of money

| Old Money | 6d. | 1s. 0d. | 2s. 6d. | 3s. 4d. | 6s. 8d. | 10s. 0d. | 13s. 4d. | 15s. 0d. |
|---|---|---|---|---|---|---|---|---|
| New Money | 2½p | 5p | 12½p | 16-17p | 33p | 50p | 66-67p | 75p |

# LTVAS GROUP PUBLICATIONS 2006

SO DRUNK HE MUST HAVE BEEN TO ROMSEY     £1.90
(A history of Romsey's Pubs and Inns, 1st Edition)     *out of print*

A SLICE OF OLD ROMSEY     75p
(Photographs of Romsey 1860-1945)     *out of print*

OLD ROMSEY AT WORK     90p
(A History of Industry and Transport in Romsey)     *out of print*

DRAWING THE MAP OF ROMSEY     30p
(The Development of Waterways and Roads)     *out of print*

WHEN THE NUNS RULED ROMSEY     90p
(Aspects of the History of Romsey in Saxon and Medieval Tomes)     *out of print*

ROMSEY REMEMBERS     £1.25
(Personal Reminiscences)     *out of print*

A TOUR OF OLD ROMSEY     E1.80
(The Appearance of 19th-century Romsey)     *out of print*

WELLOW THAT WERE     £1.90
(Memories of Wellow)     *out of print*

WHEN THE MAMMOTH ROAMED ROMSEY     £2.00
A Study of the Prehistory of Romsey & District

THE STORY OF ROMSEY     £3.50
    *out of print*

SIR W.P. OF ROMSEY     £2.95
(Sir William Petty, 17th-century polymath, colleague of Pepys)

ROMSEY SCHOOLS, 900-1940     £3.50

THE FIVE HIDES OF NURSLING     £6.00

ROMSEY MILLS & WATERWAYS     £5.95

ROMSEY: YESTERDAY & TODAY     £5.95

THE HISTORY OF ROMSEY     £7.50

BRADBEERS: The Story of Romsey's Departmental Store     £7.50

REV. BERTHON: Builder of Collapsible Boats     £5.95
(The Story of Romsey's 19th-century vicar and businessman)